THE
VISION

OUT-OF-BODY REVELATIONS
OF DIVINE WISDOM

JAAP HIDDINGA

BOOKS

Winchester, UK
New York, USA

Copyright © 2005 O Books
O Books is an imprint of John Hunt Publishing Ltd., Deershot Lodge,
Park Lane, Ropley, Hants, SO24 0BE, UK
office@johnhunt-publishing.com
www.O-books.net

Distribution in:
UK
Orca Book Services
orders@orcabookservices.co.uk
Tel: 01202 665432 Fax: 01202 666219 Int. code (44)

USA and Canada
NBN
custserv@nbnbooks.com
Tel: 1 800 462 6420 Fax: 1 800 338 4550

Australia
Brumby Books
sales@brumbybooks.com
Tel: 61 3 9761 5535 Fax: 61 3 9761 7095

New Zealand
Peaceful Living
books@peaceful-living.co.nz
Tel: 64 7 57 18105 Fax: 64 7 57 18513

Singapore
STP
davidbuckland@tlp.com.sg
Tel: 65 6276 Fax: 65 6276 7119

South Africa
Alternative Books
altbook@global.co.za
Tel: 27 011 792 7730 Fax: 27 011 972 7787

Text: © 2003 Jaap Hiddinga
Originally published as Visionen en uittredeingen by Ankh-Hermes Publishing
© 2003 Uitgeverij Ankh-Hermes bv, Deventer, the Netherlands

Design: Jim Weaver Design
Cover design: Krave Ltd., London

ISBN 1 905047 05 3

A CIP catalogue record for this book is available from the British Library.

Printed in the USA by Maple-Vail Manufacturing Group

Contents

Introduction

Most of us have heard of out-of-body experiences. We may even know people who claim to have had them, but we don't think of them as "real."

Most of us don't understand what actually happens when we have such an experience. In its simplest form, the soul, the only true entity within yourself which is everalsting, leaves the body for a while and can journey through other dimensions of life which are normally not visible for us. During such a journey the soul may receive lessons and experiences which are beyond the realm of normal life and may bring an awareness of the greatness of the creation on all levels of existence. We can even experience it without being aware of it. Just as with dreams, it can be difficult to retain a conscious memory of it after we wake up, or go back to our body.

But its influence can play a significant role in our lives, far more than we generally recognize. The experience is still "there," in our subconscious. Both dreams and out-of-body experiences appear to be mechanisms that help us in our daily routine, and we often feel calmer and more relaxed afterwards. Something has happened to us during that period, which has changed our perspective on things. We all know the old saying: "I'd better sleep on it before I make my decision." It suggests that somehow a process during our sleep will change our perspective.

But while most people can remember their dreams (though the degree to which they can do so varies significantly) only a small number can remember out-of-body experiences in a conscious way. I don't know the reason for this, but, counter-intuitively, perhaps it's something to do with the fact that during the out-of-body experience, the visions are more realistic. The images in dreams are obscured by all sorts of symbolic meanings, and therefore they are not as probing. What we see during an out-of-body experience can be very strange, and sometimes wholly unacceptable to our way of thinking, while dreams are somehow "softer," more manageable. Perhaps we are protected in a way to only allow in those images that we can mentally accept. Nevertheless, both are experienced in equal measure, whether we know it or not.

There are similarities between the two, and sometimes they may overlap. But there's also a key difference. In a dream the soul does not leave the body. It may receive knowledge from another level of existence, but, because it is still attached to the body, no images are available to create a coherent picture. The brain simply scrambles the information and uses whatever images are stored during a lifetime of experiences. The result is often a "story," which usually appears illogical. In this story you might play a role, a bit-part. During an out-of-body experience the soul actually leaves the body and journeys into an unknown world, where it can receive information in the form of teachings. Sometimes this is expressed as a "vision." But, in contrast to a dream, you are fully aware of taking part, and observe everything in the same way as with daily life.

It's a useful exercise to try to remember dreams, and write them down. You will train your memory to recall those hidden experiences. Over time you will find it easier. Most dreams are simply processes during which the events of the day are re-organised and re-shaped. But sometimes we have dreams which have a deeper meaning and they can provide us with information about certain aspects of our life and how to deal with or even change them. Dreams with premonitions are also possible. As you get more practiced at recalling them, you may well remember other experiences as well. You may recall out-of-body experiences. To some people this comes easily. They have no difficulty whatsoever in processing these paranormal experiences.

But for others, it will require a certain amount of training and learning to understand how to deal with it.

My own experiences began at a very early age. I often saw strange things, which fascinated me and stimulated my thinking. As a child of 6 or 7 years old, before I fell asleep, I sometimes saw the most wonderful symmetric color patterns on substances I was unable to describe, as they were unfamiliar to me. I told my parents that I saw oil, which caused a bit of a stir with them. Why oil you would probably ask. Very simple. During the day I walked to school and passed an industrial area, where there were often diesel spills on the ground. When the Sun hit the spills after it had been raining, the light refractions caused beautiful color patterns. Since I had no idea what I saw before I went to sleep, I simply called the color patterns oil. Having no comparable reference in my daily life for what I saw meant I had to fall back on a less than accurate description. This lack of referents is a significant problem in relating paranormal experiences.

The person who has had the vision has to fall back on phrases such as, "It looked like," or, "It appeared to be," and describe the experience through objects or situations with which the listener will be familiar. This is not new. In scriptures such as the Bible, or the Koran, experiences of various prophets often seem incomprehensible, but, if one reads very carefully, it becomes clear that the prophet has used alternatives to describe what he has seen. The visions of Ezekiel, for example, are full of expressions like, "It looked like," and, "It appeared like." It is a misreading for these words to be taken in a literal sense. Prime examples are in the Revelation of John. The prophet had a series of experiences, but neither logical explanations, nor language to link them to his normal life. He simply had no words for them. Despite this, he tried to record the experiences to the best of his ability. However the book of John's Revelation has remained obscure, and the numerous attempts to make sense of it have led to probable inaccuracies, and, in some cases, have caused panic among those who took the suggested explanations literally.

Not all images are incomprehensible, and most experiences are easier to describe. As a child I often saw images of wars, sometimes with the most appalling scenes, which I then made drawings of. This surprised my parents, as I was not born during the war and, as a child, had not heard much about it. Not all the scenes I saw at this time were war related. Sometimes they were of disasters and accidents. Other experiences contained prehistoric animals, which we call dinosaurs, although at that time I did not know of their existence. Only later at school did I learn of these creatures. Although the images were clear enough, I did not understand them. It took some time before I knew what they meant.

Over time these images became more intense, and lasted longer. By the time I was 15 years old I regularly had visions and out-of-body experiences, during which my spirit could travel to places of which I had no knowledge. The experiences always came spontaneously and at any time of the day. Their duration varied. Some lasted only a few minutes, some more than an hour measured by normal time, but could last several days measured in the time of the experience itself. Out-of-body experiences generally last for the longest amount of time – sometimes several hours. At the beginning of the experience I am still aware of my surroundings. I can hear people talk, or the telephone ring, but I am unable to react to it. After that I move away. I feel that I leave my body, and I am always able to look at it. This leaves me feeling very humble. The human body seems so incomplete and so pitiful.

Over the years I have had several thousand experiences. Most of those are personal and contain elements that I take as lessons, or answers, to specific questions I am grappling with. Some of them are of a more general nature and contain a message, which may be of importance to those who have taken their first steps on the path to spiritual awareness. This book contains a number of those experiences. It is my conviction that they were not meant only for me, but could be of value to other searchers. Some of these experiences contain elements I cannot describe, and, where this is the case, I have indicated it. I have purposely not provided any explanations or any conclusions to the experiences, since it is not my place to do this. I too have many questions. The experiences have been recorded just as they were received. Each individual can take out of them what he or she requires.

v i s i o n

The awareness of Christ

One experience I had many years ago was during a Christmas Eve service in 1988. I was only partially listening to the Gospels and to the carols. Their habitual familiarity was vaguely depressing.

Suddenly a strange feeling came over me. A bright golden light appeared which made everything disappear, and an angel led me to a landscape somewhere in the Middle East roughly 2000 years ago. Almost simultaneously four boys were born. They were born into normal families with brothers and sisters. Their circumstances were difficult. None of the families were rich. The boys all had different abilities, and, at that moment, no contact with each other. The mothers of the boys had no specific gifts. They were happy to be mothers, and had been filled with joy, light, and happiness from the onset of pregnancy. The conception of the children had taken place in the natural way, but at the moment of the fertilization, a beam of light had descended from Heaven to the cell, to surround it with a strange light. I saw that at the other end of the cord of light a soul was waiting for the moment that the body would be ready for it. There was a different soul for each of the four boys. I watched these souls, and I could see not only their history, but also their future. I saw their many existences, and something was made clear to me, which made a deep impression and surprised me. When they were born, they were each given a name, but not one of them was named Jesus. One of them would only get that name later.

The boys grew up in a relatively protected and safe environment. The country in which they lived was part of the Roman Empire. This resulted in unstable domestic politics. People were resentful of the occupation of their land. The boys lived a normal life; sometimes they were depressed, and sometimes happy. But, as they grew up, it began to emerge that they were different from their contemporaries. They were very serious young men. Because they had an interest in philosophy and religion, they were taken into a community, whose purpose was to develop and spread spiritual ideas. This was dangerous, not only because of the Roman occupation, but also, because it was new. The people of this land had traditional religions, gods, and superstitions, and there were many priests who saw this group as a danger. I was not familiar with this group despite my knowledge of the history of this era: they were not Essenes, nor Zealots, nor any other name I recognized. The group had originated from the area near Babylon, and it was already more then 6000 years old. The group was persecuted, because it was claimed that they used magic forbidden by Jewish Law.

The boys learned and, under the guidance of their teachers, they began to develop special gifts. Their teachers knew why these four had incarnated on Earth, but did not divulge this to them. Various tasks and exams were undertaken, and they learned many lessons.

A special atmosphere surrounded them, when an angel came to say, "The world will experience many changes. Humanity will now harvest that what it has sown. Freedom is at hand, but first humanity will go through a dark period. It is therefore important that a divine message is given to the world, and to this end, divine awareness has been granted to you. Your role is to tell the world that divine love is in everything alive. Open yourself, and let the divine spirit enter. Go into the world, and educate, because the storm is coming."

The group was deeply touched and, immediately, a light was placed in the four men, and they acquired talents they had not previously had. Other members of the group experienced enlightenment and, in some cases, received divine gifts as well.

The angel said, "The divine spirit has now entered your body and this spirit (Christ awareness) will teach mankind many lessons. You have a great deal to do, and this is not an easy task. There is a lesson for each of you, because you must remember you are not Christ, and you have your own lessons to learn and to experience. This is more difficult than you may think, and it is also different for each of you. Do you understand this?"

The men said they did, and the angel continued, "As a human being you now have the awareness of Christ because you have chosen this. It is not your purpose to identify yourself with this awareness, because it is a gift of God, which is essential in bringing His message into the world. Go forth and carry out your task. You will receive help, and while you will be well received, you will also find humility. Once your task is complete, the awareness of Christ will leave you again, and you can continue your life, but not before God permits it."

The four men were deeply affected. They were silent for a long time, thinking about what the angel had said. From the history of the group, they had been able to read that already, long ago, there had been a prophecy that something would come, which would bring the love of God to this world. They thought that it had finally come. They were very enthusiastic, and decided to start work straight away. The four men thought that it would be wise if each of them went in a different direction. Before they could do so, there were months of training ahead. During these months, they preached and taught the News. This took place in a small-scale way, because the country was sparsely populated with little villages and towns. It struck me that although the preaching did not seem to involve much of what is written in the Bible, it did contain the simple messages of love and hope. For the first time a message of this nature went out to the poor people of the country. Those people had a difficult existence and no education, and they did not always understand the message. They lived by the old ways and were superstitious. Some of them hearing the new message thought that they would be freed from earthly oppression, while others felt the hope and the love. Their lives were different from ours – more basic, dominated by their first priority: food and survival. Many had never been cared for, and they had never learned to understand spiritual messages. The priests saw them as unimportant, and had not bothered with them. They felt alone and left out. The new message drew quite a following, and many people felt elevated by the meetings they attended.

The group was busy writing spiritual messages, visions, and lessons, which were given by the spirit of Christ. Many parchments were written.

Years passed, and the men were now grown up and ready. By giving lectures and preaching the message, their self-confidence had increased, and the awareness, given to them by God, helped them in their goals.

The time had now come to spread out and take the message into the world. One went east and traveled among the people in Mesopotamia, Persia, India, and Asia. There the message was brought into line with the background and culture of these people. Another went west, and shipped himself with a small group of followers to the continents of America. The message he took blended with the existing cultures of the people already living there. The third left the group, and traveled south, bringing enlightenment to the people of Ethiopia, Sudan, and other North African tribes no longer in existence. The fourth stayed with his followers in the area where he had started, to complete the work there. He traveled in this vast and heavily populated area, through the countries we know as Egypt, Arabia, Jordan, Iraq, and Lebanon, and everywhere the message was warmly received by the people, who felt society had left them out. Some of the people started to protest, speaking out against the ruling class of priests. Not surprisingly, these activities were not popular. The priests felt robbed of part of their authority.

The men did not notice these problems, and went on their way. Their behavior was that of wise men, who could bring to people the feeling of divine love. This was a concept previously unknown to mankind. Yet these men were themselves not strangers to normal human feelings, emotions, and problems, and sometimes their goals brought conflict within them. The normal dilemmas and struggles of human beings were well known to them, and they were no saints. The two men who had traveled to the east and west each had their own problems, because the cultures and background of the people were so different. They did not lose contact with the original brotherhood, and they exchanged messages regularly. However they never returned to their homeland. They married and died in the countries to which they had brought the messages, and where they had built their lives. I saw each man live his life, and I knew that they would meet as a group, in the future.

The man who had stayed in their homeland had many problems. Wherever he went he was persecuted. The ruling class of priests, and the occupiers of the country, noticed that a lot of good had been done, and were afraid that this movement might become so popular that it would become politically dangerous. It was not long before the man was arrested and imprisoned. During the interrogation he was misunderstood, and sentenced to death. The execution was a normal one for that country. He, together with two others, was nailed on a wooden cross, shaped like a T. They were then left to die, and the dry heat of the day, as well as the bitter cold of the night, meant that death would come swiftly. When the man was nailed to the cross, I could almost feel his pain, although it did not last long because spiritual help came. At that moment, something wonderful happened. The man had been sentenced to death because he had the divine Christ within him. He wanted to express this, but as the last nail was hammered into the body on the cross, a light came from Heaven and the awareness of Christ, which had been in him for years, left him. His task as a teacher was over. At the moment that the spirit of Christ left him he felt suddenly weakened. He collapsed in enormous pain and sadness.

A shock went through him and he shouted, "My God, My God, why have you forsaken me?"

As he was dying, he suddenly realized the meaning of what had happened. God appeared to him in the shape of a flame, invisible to the humans, who experienced His presence only as an unearthly heat spreading across the place where the crosses stood.

The Creator said, "I have never left you, and will never leave you. But in the past you have left me."

The man saw his eternal life, and admitted that during this existence he had not always been fully in tune with divine love. He saw that during previous existences he had brought trouble, death, and sorrow to many people. He had been a feared man, who did not know love, and had betrayed God many times in some extreme ways.

The Creator went on, "As you can see, you have experienced and learned much. You have brought life to Earth, but you have also taken it away many times. This life as a spiritual teacher and messenger was your task to provide the first steps for humanity to a new future. You have brought a message of divine love and life to this place, where you had brought death and sadness. You have been able to experience the divine gift in the shape of the spirit of Christ, or the awareness of Christ, and you brought hope to the people. This awareness also led to your earthly punishment and sentencing, and since you experienced this as Christ, you have exonerated your own past, and the slate is wiped clean. You are now welcome in Heaven."

The man realized the enormous lesson he had just learned. By bringing a message of love he had been able to understand this, and at the moment he died he spoke, "It is completed."

The enormous amount of karma, which he bore as a soul, was now wiped away, and he was ready to continue. The corpse was taken from the cross, wrapped in cloth and buried according to the customs of that time. The soul, which was now freed to return to its spiritual habitat, was stopped for a moment and an angel said, "You are not yet finished. You must give a message to those who were working with you, and loved you, so that they can continue to spread the work, and the message. If you go now directly to the spiritual habitat, then all the work will have been for nothing."

He watched helplessly, as his body was removed two days later. The position of the grave was now public knowledge, and his followers were afraid that the grave would be desecrated. His body was interred again at a spot nobody knew, and it has never been found. As a spirit he appeared a few times to his followers, with the message that the work that had been started must be continued. His followers each took a task, and the original group went on its way to bring the message of divine love to mankind.

A few hundred years had now passed, and I saw that the message in its simplicity was still alive, but there was something strange about it. The original followers of the four men had now passed away, but the message had continued with new followers. These people did not have spiritual awareness, and had not experienced the original events, so had no clear idea of the truth. The original message, which had been written down, was no longer public, but I saw the scrolls and parchment buried at a spot, which has never been found. I saw many watered-down versions of the message, and I saw that many churches and world leaders altered the message to their own ends. The message and the stories of the original group were now almost forgotten. Only small fragments, which suited those in power, were kept. This knowledge was used politically, and much of it was exploited as a replacement for the old-world gods, who no longer held people in thrall. The old Rome was collapsing, and the message was now used to build a new Rome. The same lies and the same nonsense, but with Jesus and disciples, instead of Venus, Mars, Astarte, and the other gods.

Again centuries passed, and I saw many monks with books which they called the Bible, but which only contained small fragments of the message, in the form of badly written Gospels. I saw that the name of Christ was used to carry out hideous crimes, and the days were dark. Finally I saw the present day, and I saw many churches, with people dancing, singing, and calling out the name of Jesus. "Jesus loves you. He will save you. He has taken away your sins," they sing.

I watched with disbelief this twisted version of the message, which had now lost all its original value. As a group, 2000 years ago, the message for the future had been given of hope and love. It had nothing to do with taking away sins and saving mankind. I watched this all with incredulity and I could not continue.

At that moment the angel appeared. "You have seen something which mankind does not understand. Two thousand years ago there were four people who, because they did this voluntarily, but also because they had lessons to learn for themselves, brought a message of divine love.

"Humanity has not understood this event. All that happened was the invention of a new religion, which made use of the main players, Jesus and Maria, and worshipped them as God. God, however, has often been forgotten. The event was important, but not in the way people think. Only a simple message of love was brought because that was what the world needed. The real events have yet to take place. There will be no second coming of the Christ as people imagine, since he has never walked the Earth as an individual, but only as a divine awareness or spirit, which is present in every human being from the moment he or she will grant it access. This spirit waits patiently for a long time, until humanity is ready to do this.

"Christ is not a living person of flesh and blood. There have never been any sins taken from humanity because no one is ever responsible for one's sins except oneself. Only Man himself is responsible for his own deeds, and one cannot transfer sins to another human being, or God. You cannot trade in sins, guilt, or mistakes, and you cannot buy yourself free. You have to do all the work yourself. Each person will harvest what he or she has sown during many ages, and each soul will be called to account. Do you understand?"

I understood this fully, and I saw that everything was different from what I had been led to believe. The path to the real light had always been there, and the divine leader had always provided help and insight. But because no one took any real interest, and was unable to see spiritually, it was easy for everything in the material world to be manipulated. I saw that a lot of people, and vast amounts of money, were sacrificed on wrong ideas. Poor people who did not have a lot to eat were forced to give up their crops and money for all sorts of misleading stories. Beautiful, but also pointless, cathedrals were built. Beautiful pieces of art were made, but those who did this out of love for their Christ were often not paid for their work, and died of starvation. The spirit of Christ was certainly not in any of these churches, cathedrals, or artifacts, and no love of divine powers was present in the pieces of wood and bone, kept as priceless religious relics. As I looked I was deeply touched, but also filled with sadness. Was this really humanity and was this all that was left of it?

The angel looked on me in a friendly way and spoke softly, "You know where your future now lies. Humanity thought that this was resolved 2000 years ago, but in reality, hardly a start was made. These four and their group were only few of the many, because in a number of countries with just as many cultures, enlightened souls have been born. Many have done their work in a hidden way, without making any fuss, and have tried to give love, light, and wisdom to those in their surroundings who needed it. Only in such an act can one recognize the true Christ. So far humanity has approached this wrongly, but this will now change. If you have seen this vision correctly, then you can understand everything.

"You also have to assist and bring light and love. Your soul knows your duty, but you are not ready yet. This will come in time. You will experience a difficult period but you will get through it unscathed. Keep faith and you will receive many gifts, which you may use to lighten your path. It will often be dark."

I was silent, deeply impressed. I was also very shaken. At that moment I heard strange music, and I discovered that I was still in the church, and I gazed wonderingly at the enormous Christmas tree.

The soul and the influence of culture

I was taken to a point outside the Earth's atmosphere, from which I could see the whole planet. It was familiar to me from the movie images taken by astronauts. There was, however, a strange mist over its surface. It was not clear, as one would expect.

The angel who accompanied me said, "You are now ready for another lesson. Although you already know some elements of what you are going to be taught, it will nevertheless be a revelation. You will see life in the material world, which will make clear to you that mankind has a great deal to learn. Watch very carefully, and remember to ask if you have any questions."

I looked at the planet, and suddenly saw billions of people walking, working, sleeping in little houses on small pieces of ground, to which they had clamped themselves in a way they perceived as necessary to living. I saw that they all identified themselves with their background. Small groups of people labeled themselves Jewish, Christian, Hindu, Islamic, Communist, Capitalist. Not everyone had such a label: some people did not care about anything at all. I saw rich people and poor people, criminals and others who strove to do well. I saw white men and blacks, the peoples of the Orient, Indians – every race indeed known to mankind. It was a very colorful spectacle.

The angel laid her hands over my eyes, and through their warmth, I felt my eyes change.

"Watch carefully," she said.

I looked again at the drama of life in front of me, and saw the souls living in all those people. I could see clearly each individual soul, and the differences in their development. But the most important fact was that every soul, despite the different stages they were at, was identical in structure. They were all divine, and originated from the same source. They were truly brothers and sisters, although the individuals did not recognize this. They fought continuously over each other's property or beliefs. The strangest aspect of this was that they identified themselves only with the cultural background into which had been born. This they took as a reality. The Jew fought the Moslem, and the Christian fought the "non-believer." The whites and the blacks fought. And all of this despite the fact there was no absolute reality to the word "Jewish," or "Christian," or any other label for that matter. These words represented only material ideologies and ideas, but they were protected as if they were something special. Color and race had no real meaning, since the soul inside the body was just like any other soul. I watched and saw that as soon as the bodies died, the souls, depending on their development, were taken to different environments. Only a vague memory was left of their body, and the souls discovered that what had been defended with zeal, came to nothing.

The angel spoke again, "As you can see, man identifies himself only with the material world, and attaches too much value to it. The souls and their divine background are ignored. It will take a very long time before mankind will awaken to this awareness, but awaken it must.

"Most of the problems on Earth, or other planets for that matter, are due to our belief that only the material body is considered to be reality. The soul is not acknowledged, and people see enemies, where in fact there are really only divine brothers and sisters.

"They fight each other over color, race, class, and religion, but these are only cultural man-made patterns. Ironically there is in this an opportunity for many lessons. Instead there is sorrow. The souls, however, are always divine, and there are no specific Jewish, Christian, Hindu, or Islamic heavens. Such a concept is the product of man's imagination. There is no heaven for blacks, nor one exclusively for whites. Only divine love counts in the real Kingdom of Heaven. Do not look at material bodies as others do, because divine love and divine laws function differently from mankind's notion.

"One will harvest what one sows. Think carefully if you condemn a person for race, class, or religion. The soul is everlasting and no human knows what the future holds. Each person will receive what he or she has done to others."

I was silent because I understood the lesson very well.

The angel continued, "Only the development of divine souls is important: not the material interests developed by groups on Earth. One will never win spurious arguments about specific ideas or beliefs, and "chosen" people do not exist. Since mankind still thinks that it can win these arguments, or be the chosen, the overall loss to humanity will be very great indeed. Everything will disappear until at last the lessons of divine love are learned and accepted."

3

The body, spirit, and soul

I was taken to a landscape, which was not at all familiar to me, although it had an earthly feel to it. Everything was orderly and neat. It was not extraordinary, and certainly not heavenly.

One of the angels who had accompanied me on earlier journeys explained, "On this journey you will receive a revelation about the human body, the spirit body, and the soul.

"As you know, the mechanism of the human body is an enigma. It intrigues many people. Humans may think themselves knowledgeable, but they do not know why the body is alive, why it is intelligent, and why it dies. There are many unanswered questions, and a great deal of misunderstanding.

"Man may think he understands psychology and genetics, but the truth is very complicated and much more difficult than human beings realize. While the material body, the spirit body, and the soul are all different, their interaction is crucial. Watch carefully, and if you have any questions, as always, please ask."

Then I saw a group of people, but what I actually saw were their bodies at work, on a molecular level.

The mechanisms of life were visible, and I saw clearly that their bodies were controlled by an energy form. The mechanical part was controlled by the brain. The impulses, which traveled through the nerves to the muscles, reminded me of telephone connections conveying a vast number of signals. The brain itself appeared to function like a microprocessor with a memory. Beyond this was another body, invisible at the material level, but bearing similarities to it. It was like an energy print of the material body, and it seemed to hold the potential for bringing the material body to life.

The angel began again, "What you see now is the spirit body, and the material body. As you can see, these two bodies are identical in appearance. It is the spirit body that provides the pattern to the material body. The brain cannot work without this spirit body, because, without it, the body would not get the information essential for growth and action. Mankind believes that the cells themselves are the biological blueprint for the body, and, on a material level, this may be correct, but not without the underlying pattern, which is provided by the spirit. In other words, the cell knows that it has to build a human being, but the spirit provides the map, or the construction drawings."

I looked further and saw that, apart from these two bodies, another body was present, but it did not look like a material and spiritual body. It resembled an energy form, with vaguely the shape of a human body. This was the soul. The soul contained everything within it, and provided information necessary to the spirit body, which in turn passed it on to the material body. Jointly they made up a living being on earth.

The angel spoke again, "The soul is the only part which is eternal, and will go through an enormous evolution. It contains everything, and will store every piece of information about every existence and every experience. The souls can therefore control the spirit, and provide the commands to build a suitable body, once conception has taken place. This is a complicated process. The right genetic conditions are provided by the parents. They are used by the spirit to build the correct body, which, in turn, is used by the soul to carry its chosen program."

I understood this, and drew a parallel with the computer. It is the hardware (or body), which requires the software (or soul), in order to do anything. This, however, cannot take place without an operating system (or spirit), to convert the signals of the software package into a machine language of the computer itself. I could see very easily all living creatures in the universe in a similar way, but this appeared not to be the complete story, because my attention was drawn to a new scene.

I saw the same landscape again, this time with a variety of people carrying out various tasks. Some groups of people looked different. Some of them had a material body, but no spirit and no soul. Instead they had a long cord, which went up toward Heaven, or some other unspecified place. These people were not easy to distinguish from normal people, who did have a soul and spirit, because they acted in the same way. Only if one paid very precise attention was it possible to see that these bodies were empty. The eyes were empty. They had no depth, and the behavior of the people was without sincerity. Yet they were happy, and took part in the activities of people with soul and spirit. Not only groups, but individuals too, stood alone, their long cords reaching to Heaven. They looked like dolls with a remote control.

The angel said, "These human bodies are indeed kept alive and controlled by other forces. They are creations, whose purpose is to provide lessons to certain people, but without inducing guilt or karma. The conception of such a body is identical to that of any other body on this planet, but instead of connecting with a soul, its existence and growth are controlled by another force. Watch carefully and I will show you an example."

I looked at the landscape, but this had now changed. On a mountain road a bus was being driven. It was so badly maintained, that it was not suitable for the heavy journey through the mountain slopes. The engine was overheated, and the driver was tired. He had not slept very much, because his boss had told him to hurry, as a great deal of money was at stake. On the bus were children and teachers, taking part in a school trip, and they were having fun. It struck me that none of the children had a soul: all of their bodies had a cord, which went up toward Heaven. Suddenly the coach blew a tire and the driver lost control of the wheel. The bus veered off the road into a ravine, and all its occupants, the children, the teachers and the driver, were killed. The souls of the driver and the two teachers were taken by other souls, but beyond that nothing happened. Spiritually speaking there were only three people on the bus, but in the material world, it was a different matter. The coach accident had disastrous consequences. The coach operator, who had tried to save money, went into liquidation as a result of the high fines, and the owner went to prison for a short time, as a consequence of his liability. The parents of the children suffered the trauma of guilt, sorrow, and sadness. These were some of the lessons ascribed to them.

The angel explained, "As you can see, all of those involved, except the children, had to learn a major spiritual lesson. By letting the children live by other divine forces, the other souls (the boss of the company, the parents, the driver, etc.) had the opportunity to learn and experience this lesson, without harming the children. Yet the accident was experienced as real. The bereaved families had the same sadness, and they have learned the same lesson. Not in every case, however, does it work this way. Indeed sometimes the opposite takes place. Watch carefully."

I looked toward the landscape, and it had changed again. This time there was a concentration camp with many prisoners, all with a soul and a spirit body. The prisoners were forced into slave labor, and those who were unable to endure this any more, or were unsuitable for this work, were killed immediately and thrown into a hole in the ground. On it was a gate surrounded by light, and there hovered many angels to take all the souls freed from their material body, and help them toward the spiritual habitat. Every soul was greeted with joy and love. This process was almost continuous because the camp was a slaughterhouse. The camp guards and the commander, however, had no soul and no spirit, but I saw yet again the same cord, which came from their bodies and went upwards. They were without souls, and simply carried out commands, which passed through the cord to the body and the brain. If such a body died, only the cord was broken, and the body was thrown away.

The angel spoke again, "As you can see, this is not a nice situation. It brings pain to people who have to experience this. Yet they do not receive this treatment without a reason: many lessons have to be learned."

I could agree with this, because I saw the eternal souls and histories of the prisoners, and understood precisely that they indeed had to experience this, before they could continue their evolution.

The angel continued, "These lessons are not easy, but to provide the conditions for this is even more difficult, and there are few people on Earth who are really suitable. As you can see, these lessons are carried out by people without souls, but who are controlled by another force. This is not always the case because, in fact, many crimes have been committed by people with a soul, who did so out of free choice. Their time will come, and God will provide for them this difficult lesson as well.

"One often thinks that major crimes are committed by psychopaths, or people with a mental disorder, but that is often not the case. A disturbed individual can commit many serious crimes, but is unable to do so for long. His very behavior and disturbance get in the way. Your history often mentions disturbed people, such as some of the Roman emperors, and other worldly leaders, but their imbalance is only gauged against the norms you have today.

"The truth is often different, and more complex. At any rate, it is not good to think in terms of 'disturbed' and 'crazy' behavior. The total sum of the spirit, the soul, the body, the task, and the assistance that is given, determine the behavior of the individual, and that is very important. If real disturbance took place, as mankind often thinks, God would act immediately because nothing happens without His permission. Mankind lives through many lessons, and the lesson of such leaders is one of them. As you know, God has never permitted a king or leader to stand above men, but God commanded humanity to live life and to work with God in their hearts. In the past this was often the case. A leader was only chosen for a short time, if the circumstances, such as war, necessitated it. However, mankind allowed these leaders to stay on, and so became enslaved in feudal systems. The people paid a high price to have a king or leader. Ultimately this is not allowed because no single human is allowed to force his will and rule over others. The lessons are clear, however, and you can see throughout history there have been many kings and leaders, who were really not suitable for the job. A lot of sorrow has been brought on to mankind, sorrow that was not necessary, because material and spiritual leaders have fooled mankind. This is the most significant lesson that humanity has to learn, and as long as it is kept this way, the lesson will continue. The lessons that men have experienced during any of the wars have been initiated by their own choice. Only God is your King. This has been sensed by mankind and, as a result, people have rebelled against the old system of kingship. This has led to various revolutions, as you can see in history, but it has also resulted in those who replaced the kings, continuing their crimes but under a different name with different lies and causes. Spiritually speaking it does not make any difference if you are a czar or party leader, an emperor or chancellor, a king or revolutionary. The same crimes will remain crimes. During the third evolutionary period, humanity has had the freedom of choice in action. In the fourth period this will not be possible. All forms of leadership are spiritual. No one can, or is allowed to, force his will on to others."

I understood this message very well.

The angel continued, "As you can see, a 'human being' is somewhat more complicated than only the material body, which you can see on Earth. Man cannot see spiritually, and therefore views all creatures as living, while often they are not. As you can see, there are many forms of lessons, but since some of them are very difficult, the Creator provides the opportunity to learn them in different ways. Everything is possible, but you cannot always see a human being in the same way as you have been used to. Some people do not have a soul and spirit body, but are there to provide opportunity and experience for others.

"Think about this and do not condemn. Remember also that the examples, which I have used here, are only examples. They only express possibilities. In reality there are many complicated issues, each different, and you can never use these examples to explain everything."

I thanked the angel for the lessons. It was clear to me that in the near future there would be another kind of revolution, which would free humanity of all forms of worldly power and leadership.

Other life forms

I was taken further into space, and again an angel who I recognized accompanied me. As we traveled, we talked. After a while the angel said, "Because you have been working on this subject and expressed a wish to know more, a journey and a lesson are provided for you. You will eventually learn about the nine dimensions, which will provide most of the answers. For the moment here are some manifestations of the Creator, which will explain more then a dry series of statements.

"There are many mysteries in the universe. The Earth and its direct surroundings are only a pinpoint in the universe and, as you know, there are many universes. It is not easy for men to recognize and then accept this, because your way of thinking and your background often makes it impossible. What seems death for you is on a different level often life, and vice versa. Watch carefully."

After a long journey we came to a strange planet. It looked unusual, with colors I did not recognize. It had an apparently chaotic landscape with a specific beauty, but not like anything on Earth. The planet was in a solar system far away, and the star, which gave it life, was very small and very brightly lit. The color was almost light blue, and the light burned everything in its direct path. We went to the surface of the planet. It is not possible to provide any real picture of this. Although it looked wild, there was an enormous amount of peace and beauty.

I asked the angel if this planet was inhabited and she answered, "Watch carefully."

I saw something move. Two enormous "rocks" (that is how they can best be described) in front of me moved slowly. I was a little shocked but composed myself again. A voice came from the "rocks" asking me who I was, and what I came for. I said that my goal was to seek out all forms of living matter, and to learn. One of the rocks replied that, as a group, they did not mind showing me some of their life.

The angel said, "Before you view their life I will provide you with a little explanation. The life you now see is real, and exists in your own matter [see Vision 13, The nine dimensions]. You will find here the same elements as you find on Earth. As you know, life on Earth is based on the element carbon. This element is the carrier and it, in combination with other elements, forms your bodies. Carbon, however, is the main element. This is not the case on this planet, however. Carbon is rare, and, if it existed in pure form, would evaporate by the light of this core star. The main element here is silicon, and life takes the form of 'living stones.' Go with them and learn".

I stepped toward the rocks and, to my amazement, they moved, ever so slowly, in the direction of a strange rock formation in a variety of colors. One rock explained that this was their village or community. It appeared that they did not require a roof over their heads, and their appearance was such that they had no other technologies. They either did not need them, or could not express themselves thus. The rock explained that they multiplied themselves by means of cell division. Small blocks separated from a larger block, and grew very slowly by means of absorbing elements from the atmosphere. I had questions about physiology, organs, thinking patterns, culture, and religion, but the rock replied with some amazement that these were ideas unknown to them. My questions were obviously too much based on the way of thinking I had as a human being.

The largest rock replied, "Our bodies have no internal organs, as you understand them, and therefore you cannot view our life in the same way as your own. Our molecular structure provides an answer as to how we live, think, memorize, communicate, and grow. It is a complicated crystalline form of elements. These process signals in an electrical way, and thus we can store information, think about situations, and learn. We have no brain, arms, legs, lungs, or heart. We are only a complex crystal structure that is alive, and which processes information within its crystalline structure."

I thought about silicon as the base for microchips, but they cannot function on their own and require electricity. I enquired about the form of energy that provided the rocks with life, and one of them replied, "The star you see is our Sun. Its structure is somewhat different from what you are used to. The radiation has a different energy and wavelength, and you can compare this with vast magnetic radiation, which provides us with energy. This radiation is lethal for your bodies and would burn them up, but we receive our life-force from it."

I could understand this. I thought about the theories of Tesla (note xxx) who wanted to send vast quantities of electrical energy around the world without cables, by using radio techniques. Furthermore, Tesla's form of energy is harmful for our bodies on Earth. Obviously the star near this planet was in a different phase from our Sun, and the radiation was clearly much more intense and differently charged.

The rock continued, "We do not know complex culture patterns as you do, because our purpose in life is different. We cannot experience things the way you do, but we do experience everything within ourselves. Our structure, fed by the energy of our Sun, is capable of creating experiences in ourselves without the need to express this in any form."

I could understand this, and realized that some enormous lessons had to be learned by these creatures. I had the idea that they did not know these themselves, or did not want to say.

It was now time to continue and, after we said our farewell, I questioned my companion on the lessons of these life forms.

The angel explained, "As you can see, it is possible to create a living being without using any of the processes of life as you know them. There are, however, important lessons connected to this situation. Each form of life has its own lessons and experiences, but also its limitations. These limitations are not recognized until the moment that it compares itself with other life forms, and then it is aware of the differences. You also think that you have no limitations, but in reality the human body is very limited. You are able to express yourselves through emotions, feelings, ideas, and thoughts. These can range from love to hate, but also can be intellectual activities, for example, inventions, technologies, philosophies. You live in a very intense manner, or rather you think you do. The beings you have now seen cannot do this, because their bodies do not make it possible. Their structure is such that you can compare them with a living computer chip. All you do in the material world together with your work, they do, but in a world of alternate reality, which is for them true reality. In your way of thinking it can be best described as a very complex form of virtual reality.

"This of course begs the question, what is reality? The expression of reality as you experience it, or the reality as these creatures do? The truth is both are reality, and also no reality. They are only tools to learn divine lessons. You have to act to experience, but damage can be caused by the mistakes you make, and from which you have to learn. The souls of these beings, which you have now met, are from the same divine origins as yourself [see Visions 2 and 3], and are, spiritually speaking, your brothers and sisters. They have lived in other situations and on other planets. They have been brought here because in previous existences they caused problems and sadness to their fellow souls. The life form, which they have now chosen as a lesson, provides them with the opportunity to process this without doing any more damage. They have to experience these lessons for a long time within themselves."

I thought a long time about this, and I could understand it. Suddenly I remembered the old fairytales where the evil genius was often turned into stone. The angel smiled and said, "The old fairytales were not daft and certainly no fantasy. Nobody, however, understood them."

We continued our journey, and after a while arrived at a different planet, which was also very strange. There was little dry land, but what was there was divided in a strange manner. From a great height it looked like a giant cheese with many holes, which, once I was closer, turned out to be a landscape full of vast lakes. These lakes were so large there was little land visible: only a few mountains scattered among the lakes. There was vegetation, but I did not see any living moving creatures. We stood on a small hill, and looked over the largest lake in front of us.

The angel spoke, "Watch carefully and you will learn a new lesson."

As I watched, the surface of the lake moved slowly. It did not move as would happen with wind on the water, but it moved in an intelligent manner. As it did so it took recognizable shapes. A face was clearly discernible, and I found this shocking.

I looked, questioning, to the angel and she replied, "These lakes are living creatures. They consist of a liquid whose chemistry you do not know, but are formed according to another principle [see Vision 13, The nine dimensions]. The lakes contain souls from the same origin as you, and have their own lesson to learn. They have opportunities to express themselves as you would, but they cannot experience the processes of the beings you just visited. They can process experiences by receiving vibrations of other experiences. In other words they live off vibrations unconsciously created by others. It is not good to communicate with them, since this is not possible in a normal sense. If you were to do this, you would only experience a reflection of your own thinking, since that is the only thing they receive and use as life."

I found this hard to understand because if these beings only absorbed thoughts and experiences of others how did they manage to live themselves?

The angel went on, "These beings are here for a lesson which cannot be found elsewhere in the universe. This lesson is complicated and cannot be understood except through direct experience, but it has to do with absolute obedience and service to others. They can receive impressions from others from the entire universe and work with them. All thoughts and impressions are processed here and collected in these lakes."

I looked a long time in silence at the scene in front of me. The colors were strange, and I could not describe them. As the lake appeared to move and boil, it made a deep impression on me.

The angel went on. "It is time to move on because there is more to see. For the moment you are not permitted to see more details of these beings, but in the future you will meet them at much closer range."

We continued again and, after a long journey, we arrived at another planet. It looked bright in as much as it emitted light and the star of the solar system, of which this planet was a part, was very large and provided a huge amount of energy. It was very warm and we floated low over the surface without once touching it. I could, however, clearly recognize a landscape, which vaguely resembled that of Earth. There were houses, cities, and built-up areas and creatures resembling humans. The land bordered a sea, but not of water. The liquid was liquid iron.

The beings were swimming in this liquid iron, and drinking it as if it were water.

The angel explained, "This planet is so hot that all forms of life are completely different from those on your Earth. The iron, which is cold and hard on your planet, is here in use as water. The living creatures here consist of similar materials as those you saw on the first planet, but according to a completely different dimension for matter [see Vision 13, The nine dimensions]. The elements here are to some extent also available on your planet, but life is made up from many different elements. As you can see, these beings have built a sophisticated form of civilization, but they are also learning and, just like you, are on their way toward the divine light. I only show you this planet so that you can understand that life and the processes of life, matter and Earth are completely different from what you imagine. The beings you see now are alive in temperatures of several thousand degrees Celsius. In the past some of them visited your Earth by means of their technology, but the craft had an accident, and some of the beings remained on Earth. The cold (for them) meant that they could not survive, and these beings are now in a museum as unknown clay statues."

The angel continued, "Life is different from what you may think. You have now seen three extreme forms of life, each very different. As you can understand, it is not adequate to see life as only forms that are clearly recognizable, biological processes of life. Everything is alive, and this includes stones and elements, such as iron and gold. The structure of life is often not recognizable, and depends on the conditions of the planet. Many elements on Earth, such as tin and aluminum, are not available in nature in their pure form. They are connected with other elements and form minerals. If humanity wants to use them, it has to forge them from nature. They will go back to their natural state if left untreated. This you call corrosion, but it is only a process, which brings balance to these materials. Iron is alive and has its own awareness, though this is not recognized on Earth. For a large part, life depends on the energy it receives, and the expression of this life in the material world is equal to the vibration of the atom of the element, which is part of the matter. Only if the atom has stopped vibrating will matter be dead, but this does not take place in the universe. All matter is part of God's Creation and there is no death in this Creation, only life. It is not possible to kill something because death is impossible. Even if a human body dies, it is not dead. The soul will leave the body, the biological processes stop, the body does not move and it will rot away. Millions of little creatures are feeding on the remains of this body because this is life for them, and these millions of creatures, in their turn, are eaten by birds or other creatures. All is full of the spirit of God, even the hardest steel which appears dead and lifeless. If it was really dead, it would fall apart as dust, and you would not be able to use it. But life in steel is not recognized. The spirit of steel is just as real as that in you, and if you work with this spirit, you can do much more than you are able to do just now. It would not be necessary to use complicated and costly methods to manufacture steel, and you would be able to construct it to make it more beautiful and stronger. Everything in this universe is alive and filled with the spirit of God and His divine love. You call something dead because it does not react according to your own, limited, calling in whatever form. It is just as well that God does not see mankind as dead even though most of you do not react to His calling. You must therefore see life in a different way, and the definition of life as different from the definition you are familiar with."

I understood this, but had a question as a result of a discussion with someone on Earth as to whether or not the route from divine energy toward matter was reversible.

The angel smiled. "Think about the journey through the nine dimensions [see Vision 13]. The fifth dimension has been explained to you as small particles, which come directly from God. The reverse is possible but complicated. The particles get their properties from God. Those properties will determine the final shape of matter and energy, and thus its final existence. This means that if you wish to go from matter, back to this primal form of divine particles, you would have to do so with God. There is no law in physics that will allow you to do this by yourself. What came from God will return to God. Humanity cannot do this, which is why this route is seemingly irreversible. You do not have the power and permission to undertake this task. You are being allowed to play in a very simple way with the atoms of matter, and I will give you more information in the future on how you can change the whole atom into energy (what you call nuclear diffusion), but further than that you will not go, unless divine permission has been granted for this."

I understood this; obviously the whole process was reversible, but only if carried out by the Creator Himself. The angel continued, "It is possible to observe this process because it takes place in certain corners of the universe. Whole systems here are being cleared because they cannot provide for life in their present form. All matter will go back to the primal matter, the divine particle or energy quantum, and a new system will be created there. You can see this with your telescopes but you cannot understand it. In time you will."

We continued back to Earth. I thought about all I had seen. The living stones especially were intriguing. Many images and other forms on earth, as well as many old writings, came back to me.

The angel smiled again and said, "We are now at the end of this journey and the next time we will continue on other problems of physics. You have been wrestling with the so-called Revelation of John. This intriguing story is not understood by anyone for the simple reason it is not written down correctly. On your next journey this will be rectified."

Creation

I was taken into a space that was very colorful, and made up of many shapes. It was not dark, but neither was it bright. Everything was very beautiful, pleasant, and peaceful. One of my companions from previous journeys was there.

This angel spoke, "During your previous journeys you have seen many things. In many philosophies and religions there are stories about the creation of what mankind calls the universe. People have always asked questions about when and how it started, and when it will end. You will now see the creation, or rather the lifecycle, of the material worlds of the souls in what we think of as the Neutral Zone. Understanding this is not easy, and many people have searched in vain for knowledge. To you they are a multitude of planets, stars, and galaxies. Watch carefully, because the truth is different from that which people may think."

I looked, and I saw the vastness of a single universe. It was only one of the many I saw in my immediate vicinity, but my attention was focused on that specific one. I saw that it was "alive," and slowly moving. I looked further, and I saw star systems in this universe. Thousands of stars were visible as far as the eye could see.

Then I looked deeper, and I saw individual stars and planets within the systems. They too were alive on their respective levels. The angel put her hands on my eyes, and through the warmth, I could feel them change. Everything was dark now, and I could see nothing.

The angel said, "You have seen an area well known to you, but it is only a material impression of what is really there. Look again."

I watched, and suddenly I saw a vast space, the same space as before, but now filled with strange images of light, energy, and movement. Everything was moving, turning and "boiling" in a manner that I could not really describe. I saw that everything was in continuous movement, but I did not know what it was.

The angel said, "What you see is the divine process of life. Something similar takes place in your body, but on micro levels. This process of life is the eternal provider of life, and Creator of the universe. This cannot be seen by people in the material world, because it takes place at a spiritual level. If you look again, you will discover that the visible material universe is a perfect material reflection, or crystallization, of these divine processes of life."

I did so, and again I saw the divine process of life, but this time with the planets, stars, and star systems. It appeared that all these planets and stars were positioned on node points on the energy lines within the processes of life. Each time there was increased activity by these processes, a planet or a star appeared in the material universe. What I was looking at was like a giant living entity, and each time there was any activity in the processes of life something happened on the stars and planets near that location.

The angel went on, "You have now seen the connection between the material worlds and the divine processes of life. It is important now that you go back in time, and then forward, to see a section of the future."

She put her hands over my eyes again, and I saw what I could no longer recognize as a universe. The divine processes of life were re-shaping, and vast amounts of energy were contracted together in this process. The stars and star systems were born out of this. Furthermore, I could see that these processes came from the death of a previous process. All matter and energy appeared to be as one, and seemed to contract, expand again, and split. If a universe died, it seemed that all matter and energy died, and reverted to divine energy. Once the birth of a new universe took place, this divine energy split itself again in new energy and matter, and the whole process began again.

However, this was not all. I saw that each time a change had taken place, and the universe was partially renewed, some form of evolution had taken place. The energy values had changed, the energy and matter had changed, and indeed slightly improved. The divine process of life, which expressed itself in the material world in the form of planets, stars, and star systems, evolved in a way that was similar to cell division in the growth of a body. I experienced this as a revelation, because it meant that everything was subjected to growth and evolution, and that real improvement took place.

Yet this bore no resemblance to anything I knew in the material world as taught by the various astronomers and scientists. During the life of a universe continuous change took place. Planets and stars died (just as body cells which had completed their lifecycle), to be replaced by new stars and planets. This process was continuous. At no two given points was the universe the same. Consequently it could never be viewed in isolation. I also noticed the universe was neither expanding nor contracting, but gently pulsating and "living," and this I could not describe. Then I realized that I could see far into the past as well as into the future, and this too led me to the conclusion that the process was continuous.

The angel went on, "In contrast to what many people think, there is no beginning and no end. As you can see, the universe is living as a body, as a result of the divine processes of life. God was never born and will never die. The material universes within the Neutral Zone are a part of the entire Kingdom of Heaven, and they too were never born and will never die, but are continuous, and given with love by the Creator as a habitat for the souls to learn their lessons. The many changes which take place are a part of these divine processes of life, but on a smaller level, and consequently these changes are barely visible."

I looked again and saw the birth of a solar system within a star system. The divine processes of life formed a blueprint for a star and planets, and I saw that this was like a node point within the body. This node point was concentrated activity and energy, and in very colorful light. It looked like a turning wheel of fireworks of enormous size. It was beautiful. The energy began to concentrate, and slowly matter was formed. It began to crystallize or incarnate, and in the node point of the divine processes of life, a star was formed, from which the planets were born. I saw also that other stars and planets, which had previously occupied this spot, had died. From the remaining energy a new solar system was born, more beautiful and much improved. This process took place throughout the entire universe in a manner that appeared to be continuous and I saw, moreover, that it took place at every level. The whole star system, which consisted of many solar systems, was also formed in this way, and had a similar lifecycle. I realized that this was similar to many Creation myths. It was beautiful and special, and I felt love and happiness, although I could not describe why I felt this.

The angel spoke again, saying, "You have now experienced the divine processes of life. These processes create on all levels the possibility of life and habitats. In other words these processes create the areas within the Neutral Zone where every soul can, and must, learn his or her lessons. All you have seen is only an expression in spirit and in matter, of the love of the Creator. He will never leave anyone because this would mean that these processes themselves are abandoned, and that is not possible. All forms and manifestations are part of this, because human bodies also consist of the components you find throughout the universe. You exist because God exists. If these divine forces did not exist, you would not exist either. You are an expression of a part of God, just as are the Earth and the Sun. Man is in denial of these forces. He is ignorant, for denial of God is in reality a denial of the real self, and by this denial, he is cut off from the help that God is constantly providing. Do you understand this?"

I said yes, because this was not a difficult lesson, and I was very impressed by what I had seen within this enormous life cycle.

The angel continued, "This event is actually much stranger than you have seen, but it is not good to see more. In fact it is impossible. You have much to experience before you can see the rest, and that is why we go no further. Go and prepare yourself, be strong, because strange things will come to you."

6

Revelation and black holes

I left my body, and was greeted by one of the angels who had accompanied on earlier journeys.

She said, "As promised, a number of situations that have puzzled many people on Earth are now going to be explained to you. You know the book 'the Revelation of John' and since you had many questions about this, you will be given these revelations in a renewed form, visually. You will see these images in reality. Because you are now able to understand a great deal, you will be able to understand the real meaning of the revelation. Understanding John's revelation is not an easy task, and has exercised the minds of many people in research, and caused many people to be afraid. The so-called revelation mentioned terrible events, which nobody understands. This is mainly because the cultural patterns and backgrounds, as well as the way of thinking and the knowledge of the people who saw them and wrote them down, was insufficient to make sense of what they saw. People who, centuries ago, lived in peace around the Mediterranean could simply not comprehend that what was revealed could have a reality, and that the images of what they saw could be more than just visions. The viewer, the writer, the translator, and the people who have tried to explain them have interpreted the images as image, because they could not understand that some of them were real, not symbols. Watch carefully."

We floated a short time through a landscape, which, although strange, looked familiar. It had two "faces," one of which gave the impression of being beautiful, and the other very ugly.

After a while we stood still on a mountaintop (not a real mountain but it felt like one), and we looked out over a strange landscape, which resembled all the different formations of the Earth. Within one vista were all the continents, islands, and people, whose activities I could see, not only on a large scale, but also in the most minute detail. Suddenly my attention was drawn to a few specific places in this world. I saw terrible diseases. Wounds and other abnormalities were visible on the victims. Many people died. The suffering was everywhere. Some of the sick made desperate prayers to an image of God, asking why they had to experience this. At that moment another scene appeared (in this vision it looked like a second image on a different level from the one I had seen first), and I saw that these people were sick from these diseases because they themselves had worked against the spiritual and physical laws. Diseases were the result of bad eating habits, wrong sex, wrong handling of materials they did not know, such as poisonous chemicals and radioactive materials. But most of all, diseases were inflicted on purpose, by one man to kill another. Tons of poisonous gas and bacteria were stored, ready to use in biological and chemical warfare. Experiments carried out by one group of people on other parts of the population without their knowledge created enormous injuries.

Every problem was caused by the ignorance of mankind. However, the diseases were contained within small groups of people on Earth, while other groups did not appear to have any problems. I watched this image for a long time, until suddenly I saw an even larger threat. I saw a strange image in the shape of a monster, which changed slowly and grew stronger, until it was fully formed. The monster then attacked humanity with a force that was terrible in its intensity. Almost everyone suffered from its coming.

The angel spoke, "As you can see, mankind is responsible for many problems. Much sorrow is caused because many things are not fully understood, and work against the divine laws. Problems with illnesses, diseases, and painful death, as you know them, do not need to exist, but are created by mankind itself. The monster you see is real. It is a virus, which at the moment is mutating, until its final form is complete. This virus will bring the largest plague humanity has ever known, and will result in suffering in the material world. The monster is still growing. It will take a while before you will see it, but come it will. Moreover, you have to remember that humanity has made the growth of the monster possible by manipulation of illnesses and viruses, and also with medical bungling, the result of which is that the mutation will only grow more quickly."

At that moment my attention was drawn to another scene – a dead landscape: burned out tree trunks, the land black with soot, and the rivers which flowed through this, stinking, red, yellow, and brown from the various poisons in them. Dead fish floated on the surface, and the people who ate the fish became ill and died. The land did not yield crops, and people were hungry. Again there was a second scene and I saw that, yet again, the people themselves were to blame. With force all minerals and treasures had been wrought from the Earth. Many tons of poison had been dumped in the rivers, and smoke belched into the atmosphere. No one cleaned up, because no one cared about the future.

Wars with firebombs and other weapons added to the destruction, so that everything was burned, and nothing could grow. People were starving, but as a result of wars and other interests, food which was abundantly available elsewhere in the world could not reach these people, and they died of starvation. My attention was drawn by a strange image, and I saw that the landscape of the earth was "alive." It took the form of a body and a face.

The face looked at me with a sad expression saying, "I am ill, and I am dying but I will try to hold on until mankind has learned that I am not just a sphere which floats in space. I will not leave mankind until my time has come, and my Creator orders me to leave for the spiritual world. But I am very tired and have little energy left. I will not live much longer."

The angel spoke again, "The solar system will disappear – you have seen during an earlier journey how such an event can occur – but before this happens, life as you know it will disappear, to be rebuilt in another form elsewhere. This you know, so I won't have to explain it further. Life in its present form on Earth will no longer be, and, as you can see, it is mankind that is hastening the process. Life is not only something that takes place on a biological level: it is also filled with divine energy. The planet itself is alive, and you can compare this with the life forms you have seen in other places in the universe. Earth too has a soul, and it is sick and dying. This means that the biological functions on this planet cannot continue. This is a natural process, and takes place throughout the universe on each planet and star all the time. The souls of the celestial bodies, which have already died, create new habitats. You have seen this in the vision of Creation [Vision 5]. You cannot stop this process by being careful with the planet, but you can help to restore the natural rhythms and bring less sorrow to the soul of the planet by living in harmony and balance with nature, instead of bringing destruction. The planet is big, and has a huge capacity to heal itself. But it is not indestructible, and if you continually cause damage, its lifespan will be shortened dramatically."

My attention was now drawn to a completely different scene. Parts of the Earth were struck by floods, rain, storms, volcanic activity, and earthquakes. Many people experienced these "tests" and prayed to their God for help. Many people were wounded, killed, or missing.

Again I saw a second image; that while these disasters were problematic, they were only an expression of life on this planet. There were no divine mistakes in this. The balance of life was being maintained. Mankind experienced these disasters because they no longer believed in the divine hand. Rather, they put themselves and their superiority first. According to their thinking, these disasters should not happen.

The angel said, "What you have seen are situations in the past, the present, and in the future. These so-called disasters have always been there and, depending on the structure of the planet, will continue to be there, in one form or another. It is men's thinking that causes the problems. Sure, the events are not pleasant, but there are lessons connected to them. They do not come for nothing, but man's fear of losing something is very great, and this makes the events a disaster for the body instead of a blessing for the soul."

We left the mountaintop, and after a while we arrived at a different mountain, on the top of which was a small stone temple in the shape of a circle (a small form of Stonehenge), and within the circle were some benches. By then it was night, and the sky above me was dark blue. Billions of stars sparkled above my head, and I looked for a long time at this scene. It was very beautiful and peaceful.

The angel spoke again and said, "You have now seen a number of images which are similar to those that the seer saw and wrote in the book of Revelation, but what you have seen is not complete. As you can understand, the person who saw this was both terribly impressed, and upset. Yet these images do not portray the end of the world, as people may think. Mankind does not understand life in the material world and in the spirit. It has already been explained to you that there is no such thing as a God angry at His Creation. What humanity has sown during many ages, it will have to harvest. In other words, what will come has been set in motion by mankind itself. There is no anger from God, only love. Do you understand this?" I said yes because this lesson had been shown to me many times before.

The angel continued, "During recent centuries many disasters have created problems for humanity. These events had spiritual lessons connected to them. They were not punishments from God. These disasters have only touched those who had created them by their thoughts and actions. Therefore, small groups of people or even whole countries, but rarely the entire world population, have to endure these terrible events. You may also draw the conclusion from this, that if you have nothing to fear, nothing will happen to you. It is the total sum of your thoughts and actions over many centuries that is important. Your own future is locked within your soul, but it is also connected to the rest of humanity. The future, which will not be an easy one, as you will see any moment now, is made by mankind and not by God. God in His eternal love won't let humanity suffer too much in something it does not, and cannot, understand until mankind learns to live by the spirit, rather than materially. Watch carefully and learn."

We were still on the stone benches within the circle, and the night sky was still visible. Suddenly there was a light, and within this light many images were visible. I saw that the Earth had to endure many situations. I saw that a great war came, in which many countries took part, and in which many people met their material death. Next I saw a number of very large spaceships containing strange creatures, who also declared war against the people of the Earth. Next there was an enormous earthquake. One half of the planet appeared to shudder and sink into an ocean, and again I saw many people die. Then I saw the Sun. It had changed, and the atmosphere of the planet could no longer protect humanity from its deadly rays. Many people suffered wounds and burns. Many died. I saw a volcano erupting. A sea of fire engulfed everything, until all was destroyed. Last of all an enormous meteor struck Earth, and massive flood waves hammered the land. The atmosphere was polluted with dust and soot. The rays of the Sun could no longer reach the surface of the planet, and all life was dead.

A long time it was silent. Winds blew over the Earth, and nobody could live there. All plant life was dead. Nor was there any animal or human life left. After a long time the dust settled, and the destroyed planet was visible. I did not recognize it, as the continents looked different. There was land and water, but everything was barren and lifeless. Suddenly my eye was struck by something strange. In the middle of the lifeless barren gray desert I saw a small plant with two green leaves between the stones. On one of the leaves there was a little beetle (a ladybird), and I stood and watched in some amazement, but also with sadness mixed with joy.

Suddenly I heard a voice from the light, which said, "This is the future. Remember all you have seen well, for the knowledge is required at a later date. The material future of mankind is that of change and death, but the spiritual future is that of transformation and growth. The Earth will no longer remain in its old form, or provide any support to life as you know it. This is not unique. It is part of the life of the universe, which you can view every day on other celestial bodies, through a telescope. It has happened many times on Earth itself – humanity has already had to experience this more than once. The material death of mankind is not a punishment from God, but only an essential movement of evolution through life to a more useful existence. The destruction of the material forms you know is not death, but only a new beginning. The little plant you saw signifies new life, and the period that will follow can be used by mankind to develop his learning. Above all he must learn divine love, and he must comprehend that the divine spirit will provide humanity with this new opportunity. Whether the plant grows on Earth or elsewhere is not important, because grow it will. That is a promise. When this will happen is also not important. However, remember this, it can be tomorrow or in a hundred years, but I will not give any revelation to humanity as to how and when all this will happen. Be prepared and alert because I will come as a thief in the night, and I will be before you when you least expect this. I will only provide a warning in as much as you need it, and I will do this for every living being. The total sum of your soul determines which warning you will receive, and this means that no two warnings will be identical. Do not see this as a cruel punishment because that is not what it is. Rather see it as a means of help, given in divine love to rebuild everything anew in a better and fitter shape. The rubbish has to be separated from the useful. Humanity will not survive in its present material form, but will survive in spirit, to go on in a new material form, which is clean and beautiful. This is your task and complete this with great care."

The light was now fuller, brighter, and appeared to be very close. I was silent, thinking for a long time about all I had seen, and also on what I had seen during earlier journeys and lessons. I could grasp the essence of the revelation, but did not know what I had to do.

I questioned this, but the voice only replied, "Your role is not easy and you will get a lot of help. Lead people and provide knowledge, but it is not good to know more. Too much knowledge would be a hindrance in everyday life, and there are a few things that will have to be resolved before then. You would only worry about things that are not there yet. You have nothing to fear because I am always there."

The light began to disappear, and at last it was almost away. We could see that it was now almost day, because the night sky had the colors of the first daybreak.

The angel spoke again, "You have seen much and together with all other journeys, lessons, and revelations you can now piece together a complete image of yourself and the future, as well as the past. I hope that you will therefore understand the present much better. There is much more for you to experience and see."

I had some questions regarding what I had seen. I asked about the meaning of the figures and images in the Book of Revelation, because it struck me that I had seen none of these.

The angel replied, "Many of these details are only images as written down by those trying to make sense of the information. Mankind in the past could not comprehend the truth, and if the prophet did see an airplane, or something with a serial or telephone number, then this was seen as something special. Do not think in details because this often clouds the real knowledge. Such details are very rarely really important, but mankind does not understand this, and many unimportant details are often made more important than the real message itself. This message should be clear to you by now. The image of those who were marked is also clear. It has been explained to you that many situations will come, but that one determines his or her future in the total sum of his soul. This is meant by the mark. That what has been sown as human and soul must now be harvested as human and soul. One determines his or her own future and this is the image of the various figures. It is different for everyone. This means in reality that the revelation will have to be found within oneself, and not outside in disasters and chaos. Each individual bears his own revelation within, in his or her soul, and in this revelation the future of the soul is written. This may mean that an individual will lose his life along with other individuals because, for example, they were struck by a meteor, but it is also possible that this same individual will be a survivor because he was temporarily protected from this event. Do you understand this?

"The revelations are only possibilities, but mankind should not look toward these possibilities, and then become afraid. Each human being has his or her own revelation from within the soul. Even at this moment in time, humanity is still working on the total sum that determines the future. Some learn, while others do not. It is neither your problem, nor your responsibility, because it is the responsibility of each individual. If someone asks, you can show the way, but neither you nor anyone else can save the world. That is not what is meant. One has to save himself or herself, and as soon this is understood, he or she will receive all the divine help of the entire Kingdom of

Heaven. God is only Love – but not a soft option. The path through the fire is one of spiritual cleansing, so have no fear of it, even though it appears hot."

I thought a long tine about all that had been said to me, and everything I had seen. We left the stone circle on the top of the mountain, as it was time to go back.

Suddenly the angel said, "Would you like to see a real black hole? You have been busy with many mysteries, and it could be of importance that you see this and have knowledge of it."

I was surprised because I had not thought about this possibility, and I replied "yes." We traveled further through the vast universe, and after a long journey arrived at a star system where, at a certain spot, there was a strange light in the shape of two trumpets, positioned against each other. In the middle of this was darkness.

The angel spoke, "You will now see a so-called black hole. A black hole is not what your scientists on Earth usually accept. Most of them believe that a black hole is an old star, which has collapsed, and therefore will have such a mass and gravitational pull that nothing, not even light, can escape. These situations do exist, but they are not true black holes, because this idea is the product of the limited thoughts of men. It is not possible that matter will collapse completely, and that atoms cease to vibrate, without a driving force making this happen. There is always a divine force. If this force were not present, it would mean that ultimately the whole universe would collapse, and that the internal energy or entropy of the universe would be lost, and that is never the case. What you see now is a true black hole. Watch carefully because you will be able to see a lot."

I looked toward the light scenes in front of me, and I saw in the center that there was a real black hole. It was difficult to see if this was a hole, or something else, because it was just black, and there was nothing to see. The hole sucked all matter and particles into it, and it was amazing to see just how much matter there was inside. Where did this all go, I wondered.

The angel spoke again and said, "On your previous journey you have seen life forms you would not normally associated with life. I have also told you that from a divine point of view, there is no such thing as death, unless the atoms in the object no longer vibrate, and have collapsed. I have also told you that this could not happen in the known universe. This is not entirely correct, because within the vast empty spaces between stars and planets there are some gases and atoms, sometimes not more than 1 atom for each 1000 cubic meters. They are vibrating very slowly, and are therefore almost dead. In a black hole, however, matter comes to a complete standstill, and the atoms no longer vibrate. They collapse. A black hole is just like a star, or a planet, or a complete system, only another expression of the spiritual divine body, which forms the universe. Think about your journey during which you saw the pulsating universe. The function of a black hole is that of renewal. The hole can be seen as an opening which sucks up dead matter and which will be transformed into a new and better material, which will in turn create a new universe. It is a type of transformer, where mostly the fifth dimension [see vision 13] will offer new possibilities. We will now go through the black hole."

I hesitated for a moment and looked toward my companion. She assured me, however, that nothing would happen, and we went faster and faster toward the black hole. The hole did not look big, but it was really not possible to see anything, because it was just black. Although there was nothing to see, one could feel. Enormous forces pulled on all the matter, and it felt like being trapped in a whirlwind of particles from where no escape was possible. It was so completely dark around us, that there was nothing to see except ourselves. Everything felt thick and black, and it appeared that we were suffocating in the amount of matter around us.

A few minutes passed, and suddenly we came out the hole to the other side, and I was amazed at what I saw. The universe was no longer like a night sky with stars, but a sea of light with a variety of colors, and I saw that the matter which had been thrown out was forming again into living pulsating atoms and molecules, which were all bright. They were no longer dull, dark materials, but bright and renewed. All this bright sparkling dust was taken in a whirlwind, and I saw that new spiral nebulae were formed. I looked further, and I saw that these spiral systems behaved more calmly, and that new stars and planets were formed. Above all it was very bright and colorful, and there was no darkness, such as I had experienced before we went into the black hole. I looked toward the black hole, but it now looked like a bright hole, in which there was nothing to see. From this light the new universe was born.

I was deeply impressed and asked my companion how we would get back.

The angel said, "To go back we are making use of the same black hole again. You have not changed. The black hole has had no influence on you on this occasion. Come then. We will go back to your own universe."

We floated toward the bright hole, and all was a blinding white. We went inside and in a moment we were back in the known universe. Behind me I could see the black hole again. I thought a long time about all that I had seen. On close inspection it was not so strange, and it appeared that this was one of the processes by which the universe was constantly renewed and altered. A black hole was obviously a system in which matter was altered and brought back to divine energy, and then used again in a new altered form. It was almost like a reverse nuclear reaction, which created matter from old matter already dead.

We went back and the angel spoke, "I see that you have understood the black hole. You can use this knowledge in the future." I thanked the angel because I was glad that I had seen this.

The angel smiled and said, "There are many more things you may visit, if there is time. Life does not only consist of lessons that are spiritual, but if you have an interest in certain subjects, and if it is permitted, then you may request specific journeys. There is a lot to see, to learn and to experience."

Good and evil

I found myself in a very cold Portakabin, which could only be heated with great difficulty. I was pondering good and evil, positive and negative forces. I was wondering how they affected the world we lived in, the Neutral Zone. Suddenly a shining being appeared, not one whom I had met before.

This angel said, "Because you have asked, and also because you need this for the future, you will be provided with a new lesson. You will undertake a journey, during which you will see many strange things. You will see the differences between good and evil, in a way that is almost never shown to anyone. The reason you are being allowed to see this you are not permitted to know, but it has to do with your future, when you will come up against certain situations, and then you will need this knowledge."

The angel showed me an enormous wall chart, which reminded me of a family tree, but was in reality a form of hierarchy recording a company or army. On top there was a cross with a seven-pointed star, and above this stood God. Humanity too, in the form of souls from the Valley of the Souls, was in this tree. These souls could appear in many guises. They lived on a number of planets in all sorts of bodies. In the tree there were also other beings. They resembled the old forms of archangels, and gave the impression of being sub-gods. They were larger then normal souls, but smaller than God, and were responsible for all sorts of situations in the universe.

The being spoke, "As you can see, and have seen during earlier journeys, there are many souls each with their own tasks. You have seen in the past that the souls are experiencing a form of separation process, which brings them into the Neutral Zone. Once there, they will have to find their way back toward divine love. All this is familiar to you, but what you have not seen or learned, is the fact that these beings, or sub-gods, experience the same processes. They are souls, greater than complete souls, but they are certainly not God.

"At the beginning of the evolution they felt superior and mighty, and they resisted God. Although your myths say there was only one who did this, in reality almost all the sub-gods were involved. A long time ago, when the universe was not yet suitable for human or animal life, the sub-gods used the Creation as a play area, and enjoyed themselves with all sorts of nonsense. They had to incarnate, and learn, and slowly most of them found their way back to God. Once they had reached there, they were committed to help with the evolutionary process. They were the brightest angels, very great souls who assisted their human counterparts. A small number, however, did not make this journey back, but resisted the Creator. They continued to play to their hearts' content."

I saw these beings, and they gave the impression of being really big, both in form, and in energy. I saw that they were involved in strange situations on a variety of planets, difficult to describe.

Suddenly the scene changed, and I saw Earth, but in prehistory, long before human life. I saw that the planet was inhabited by an assistant of such a sub-god, one of those who resisted the Creator. This soul was not a human soul, but a soul between that of the human, and that of the sub-god. For the sake of clarity I will refer to this as a half-god.

This half-god controlled the Earth: it was his domain. He had the ability to create a type of being to assist him. His creations were small and not fully grown, but could, depending on the will of their master, take all sorts of shapes. They had no soul, but only a fabricated body with a form of primitive fabricated spirit, which translated the instruction of the master into an act. When a creature like that died, nothing was left. There was no soul, and nothing remained for the spiritual habitats. They existed on a dimension bordering on what we know as normal matter, although it was not possible for humans to see them. People, however, were seen by them.

When the first humans appeared on Earth, the ruler and his helpers experienced the presence of humans as very difficult. All sorts of problems were caused by the beings; they were real pests. Most people were concerned about them, and so the ruler changed tactics. The pests were now used to take lessons to the people but in a subtle and dishonest way, quite the opposite of what could be called divine love and divine laws.

Centuries passed, and I saw that humanity continued to be bothered by these troublesome beings. They appeared in a variety of forms, and were looked upon as gods. The creatures were excited about this, and grew cocky in their behavior. Sometimes they argued with each other for the control of a group of people. They could not bear to lose. Slowly humanity became slaves to these creatures and worshipped them as gods. People lived in fear of them, and to gain their favor they brought sacrifices, and carried out strange, unnatural practices. The creatures could appear whenever they wanted, and sometimes they did so in the shape of a religious figure such as Mary, but also sometimes as a ghost or an alien. To them this was a game. Sadly, many people saw these figures as true, and felt elevated by their belief. But none of it was truth.

The angel continued, "As you can see, the truth on Earth, and on other planets for that matter, is somewhat different from what you imagined. There is no devil or Satan who makes life a misery, but there are many astral beings that belong to the sub-gods. These beings are not real, and do not originate in the Kingdom of the Souls. They are only a creation of the sub-gods, and have caused a great deal of trouble to a naive humanity. This continues to happen, and I advise you to bear the following rules in mind. Most people are very simple when it comes to spiritual matters, and believe in what they are told very easily. The way people think often obscures reality. If humanity was further along its spiritual path, it would be able to distinguish the true angels from the untrue ones, but that is not possible at this stage of development. Watch carefully, and if you see such a situation, watch what the being asks of the people, and what is promised. If such a being promises that humanity will experience a peaceful time, that everything will come about of its own accord, and that they can prepare themselves by building a house, a mansion, or a church, do not believe these words to be true because only God can bring real peace. Everything is locked within yourself, and not in the promise of a creature who is a stranger. God does not promise anything that is locked inside you, as that would take away your free will. Future possibilities are within you. They can never be found outside. Only your own spiritual way of life determines the peace and happiness you crave. No one can ever give this to you. If you are spiritually not ready, you cannot receive. Your total sum determines your own life, and what will happen to you. Watch carefully and you will learn a lot."

I looked again toward the image, but it had changed again. I saw that the people of the Earth were busy with their life.

They did all sorts of things, unaware that they were always surrounded by the pests, who made fools of them. Not only could they see people, they could also read their thoughts. Every thought of humanity, both good and bad, was visible, and took shape at a level that people were unaware of, but was always visible to these beings. No thought was ever safe. Some people appeared to be working at doing good in the material world but, privately, in a hidden way, used their thoughts quite differently, to simulate their real desires.

These thoughts also shaped this world, and it did not matter if the actual act took place in the material world, or not. So long as the thoughts happened, they were collected and used at a given moment to disturb humanity. All sorts of appearances and images were visited on mankind, who took them seriously, not knowing that they were only shapes of their own thoughts, developed by negative forces. There were also people who believed in the devil and Satan, and carried out satanic rituals. The creatures had a lot of fun with this, and sometimes made things worse by simulating certain events.

It was frightening to see that no thought was safe.

Suddenly there was a voice accompanied by a bright light, "Why are you afraid of these creatures? They are not real, and have no part in the real kingdom. They are only a fabrication of those who have resisted me, but if you walk in my light, you play no part in their existence. They only feed themselves with the thoughts of those who give in to them, and see them as real. You have learned they have no right to existence. If your thoughts do not tend to the impure, you will be free of the influence of these creatures. This is very simple because my rules are very simple. A child can learn them. Never think that no one will see you, because I do so at all times. I am always with you, and in you, as I am in everyone, so do not hide. There is no point. As soon as you put this into practice, no real evil can harm you. There are many negative forces, but if you walk into my light, they can do no harm. Only your thinking and actions determine your life; whether it is light or darkness. There is no devil to lead you astray, if you did not decide to go astray in the first place. You always have a choice. Furthermore, I will always help you. I will not let you go, even if you decide to turn away from the light. Remember, real darkness does not exist, because it too is an illusion constructed by human thoughts."

I was silent, very impressed by everything I had seen and heard. There were many other mysteries with regard to these creatures and their negative force, but I could not really describe them. I was aware that the meaning of good and evil, and the existence of Satan, were different from what I had previously thought. The biggest enemy of humanity was its own thinking and desire. The real God was often forgotten, and replaced by thousands of unrealistic forces in the shape of creatures, all too ready to play with humanity's thought processes. And mankind took this for real.

I began to understand certain remarks I had heard regarding the power of thought, for example, that a human being could shift a mountain if he or she wanted to. It struck me as well that it was possible to experience certain atmospheres within a group of like-minded people, or in big crowds, where not only their own thoughts, but also what they had attracted in the shape of these creatures, could cause a feeling of unease. This was an enormous revelation. But there was yet more to learn.

The angel explained, "You have now seen that there are many creatures, not related to the soul, which can influence life in a strange way. Not all appearances are like this, but it is important to keep in mind that the real God does not require a big spectacle to make

Himself known. The real God has always been there, and will always be, and is present in every soul. He does not need a UFO, nor does He need the image of the four women, the mothers of the men who brought the spirit of Christ to Earth. The soul within humanity is the revelation of God Himself. And the souls, which search and are open for this, will find God in the smallest spark of light.

"Learn this lesson well. Your future depends on it. You will come up against something where your thoughts will be what is important, more so than your actions. Your thoughts can save everything, but they can also destroy everything. You will receive plenty of training, which will often be difficult and unpleasant, but is essential. Do you have any questions?"

I enquired what was coming.

The angel spoke again, "It is better that you do not know this. For the moment it would be too difficult for you to imagine, so do not worry about it. Just live your life, relaxed and comfortable. When the time comes to experience this, you will know and that is early enough."

vision

8

The meaning of Hell

I was in the space immediately around Earth, from where I could clearly observe the entire planet. With me was the angel who had accompanied me so often, and who had become a real companion. I asked why I had never seen any negative, or dark, spheres (the kind of places that we would label Hell), during my travels. On Earth I knew many myths and legends about Hell, where souls would be tormented, and all kinds of nasty events would take place.

The angel replied, "You have not seen such places, because they do not exist in God's Creation. You have only been interested in the truth of God's Creation. The infinite Creator has never created the places you describe, which is why you will never encounter them. You have now made many journeys, and learned many things, and you will have noticed an important fact. The whole universe is in a state of development. In other words, growth takes place. This is growth toward the eternal light and, in this growth phase, there are planets and souls more developed then others. Those with still some way to go will not look as beautiful as those that have almost completed their development. But that does not mean the same thing as Hell, although it may resemble it from the point of view of your human knowledge.

The kind of place you mean does exist, and indeed there are several of them, but they are not part of God's Creation. They are created by mankind. Each inhabited planet has a number of spheres

51

which function as Hell for those planets, or groups of planets. Would you like to see an example of this?"

I indicated that I would, since I was curious about how this actually worked.

The angel put her hands over my eyes, and through the warmth, I could feel my eyes change. I could see a number of different dimensions at the same time. We went to Earth, and I saw that many dimensions were running through one another, and they were all connected. After a long journey we arrived at a somber looking landscape, with a dark gray, almost black, sky. I saw from afar a kind of stone wall, which stood very tall and heavy. There was a large gate, which was closed. The angel could open it with ease, and we went inside.

My companion spoke, "Don't be afraid. We cannot be seen by those who stay here. Within this dimension we are only an energy form. They can perhaps feel our presence, but only as a warmth."

We moved forward slowly, and I beheld some form of landscape, or city, which was divided into many different segments. These segments were connected with each other, but each of them had a different structure, and it was not possible for the souls who lived here to move to a different segment. They could feel the presence of each segment, but they could not go there. Once in one of the segments, the soul remained there until it was removed, or permitted to leave by its own devices. The first segment was reasonably normal, and reminded me of some areas on Earth. Souls lived an existence here, which was very simple, and they did so in the same manner as on Earth. It was not really unpleasant here. Rather, it was a state of the unknown, and incomplete. Small crimes were committed, and life looked a bit like a bad soap opera.

The angel spoke went on, "You may imagine this as the first Hell, although this is not a good name for it. The area borders on to the first real spiritual sphere, which you have seen during your journey through the Kingdom of Heaven. You noticed that close to Earth there were various islands, created by men through their own thought, but yet still part of God's Creation.

"This area is part of the black spheres, and no true spiritual sphere is adjacent to it. From this area it is possible to evolve by learning simple lessons. As you can see, this does not happen often, since many souls enjoy being in this place, and do not attempt to leave it."

We continued our journey until we arrived again at a wall with a gate, and we went inside. The atmosphere was clearly different, and much more negative. I could distinguish many souls fighting continuously. Crimes were more serious, and in some spots, what was happening caused revulsion.

Once again the angel said, "This is now a real Hell and the souls who stay here, albeit temporarily, have created this Hell to mirror their life on Earth. This is the sphere that belongs to them, and they can do what they wanted to do, or in fact did, on Earth."

I watched with apprehension, but then we continued our journey and arrived at a new gate. We went through to a scene that was utterly revolting. Life could not be described in this place. It looked dirty. Souls looked like semi-decomposed monsters, occupying themselves with horrendous activities, and I had the distinct idea they did not know themselves what they were doing. I recognized many crimes: murder, rape, torture. I watched for a long time, for I was deeply shocked. Strangely enough, I did not feel fear, or sadness, but only a deep pity for these souls, who had chosen to be in this Hell.

We continued our journey, and again we came to a gate. Once we were through, I beheld an even more atrocious scene. It was indescribable. It was really very difficult to be there.

The angel was aware of my reluctance to go any further and spoke, "What you have seen are dimensions which really exist, and which are inhabited by souls who are far removed from the light. The spheres, or Hell, have been made by people themselves, since they have been allowed to do so. We will now experience something special. Watch very carefully, because I will introduce you to somebody, who is unknown and very misunderstood."

We continued, and floated above the Hell. I could clearly identify the seven main areas, but there were also other places, which looked strange and dark. Terrible monsters lived there. They had no likeness to anything I had ever seen or experienced. From afar I could see a tremendous castle. Strangely enough it was very beautiful. It stood right in the center of what represented Hell. I assumed this to be where Satan lives, but the angel only smiled and said nothing.

On we went until we arrived at the castle. It was a strange building, which had the potential to mirror everything in humanity.

The angel explained, "We are going to visit the person who lives here. The castle, as you can see, is very beautiful, and seems out of place in the area you have just seen, but this is only for our eyes. The souls who live in Hell cannot see this beautiful place, but only a ruin with fire and darkness, a real hellhole, because that is what they have created in their thoughts. They expect nothing less than the home of Satan himself. Pay attention because you will receive a lesson that has not previously been given to someone still in his earthly body."

We entered the castle, and I was amazed at the wonderful decorations. It was not rich and overpowering, but simple and clean. Suddenly a being of light appeared, grander than my companion, and this being approached us, looking friendly, and shook my hand. I was a little embarrassed, but our host did not notice this. We entered a large hall, and sat down on some benches. I still had not said a word although I was filled with many questions.

The being said, "My name is Nathaniel, not Satan, or Lucifer, and it is my task to govern this area. I have been sent here by the Creator to assist all their souls in their choices. It is a heavy burden I carry. It is my sad duty to help all souls in their evil, and through me many crimes are made possible."

I did not understand this, and asked if it would not be better to prevent evil from taking place, but the being replied, "You think this because you do not as yet understand evil. In God's Creation it is a right that each soul has his or her own free choice. As you have already seen it is the choice of the soul to resist the divine order, and it is this mechanism, which you have seen so often, that moves the soul from the real Kingdom of Heaven to the Neutral Zone. You also know that each soul has to make his way back to the light by means of a long and difficult journey. This is something the soul has to do by himself, and in the process is assisted by many beings surrounding him. If the souls make a choice for good, and follow the path toward God, then he or she will receive all the help required to reach this goal. All the lessons and experiences the soul will receive are designed to assist the journey toward the light.

"But in certain phases of the evolution of the soul, it is also possible to choose the dark path. A soul may want to kill someone, or torture, or rape, or commit some other crime against someone else. Logic dictates that this should be prevented, but that is not correct. You only think in the material world, but in spirit the crime has already taken place, even though you may not yet see it. At such a moment there will be many beings who will try to prevent the actual crime by sending as much positive energy as they can, but if this does not succeed, then it is my sad duty to make sure that the crime takes place. Souls do not learn by thinking things over, but by experience, and the results of that experience. Do not think that I am the cause of the crimes, for that is not the case, but I must facilitate those who exercise their free will to carry them out. I merely create the conditions so that the crimes can take place. It is then up to the soul to decide whether or not to proceed with the action. Free choice determines everything. My task is not easy, because I have to take great care that no mistakes are made. If, for instance, a murder takes place, the victim also has a lesson to learn. It is not possible to create random evil with random victims. There is a very fine balance between everything that takes place. Nothing happens for nothing. There is always a clear connection between all the factors involved. Although this is not a recognized fact on Earth, it is known spiritually, and I am the one who makes it possible. As I already told you, this task is not pleasant, and it is very lonely, but I fulfill it with love. It causes me great pain that so many still choose such destructive paths of their own free will, and I would be much happier if there were more people who would like to search for the real light. But as long as people want to make negative choices, my task is not finished."

I asked if the areas of Hell were real, and why they looked the way they did, and he replied, "All you have seen is a representation of thoughts, which those souls keep alive through their wishes. They have made a choice, and I have to help them with it. If they chose to stop making negative choices, evil would disappear within a second, and there would be no more Hell. All crime and evil would instantly disappear from Earth and other planets.

"The soul always makes the choice. No one can force it. The choices which you make are always your own responsibility and it is therefore wrong if men, who live in their bodies on Earth, call upon

Satan and blame him for all the evil they see in the world since such a Satan does not exist."

Nathaniel showed us a little place on Earth, and we could see that a small group of people occupied themselves with a séance within a so-called Satan's church. They made all kinds of signs on the floor, and carried out strange rituals. They stood blindfolded, and naked, and called for Satan.

The being looked in a sad and pitiful way to these people, and spoke.

"Here you can see the great misunderstanding. These people call for something that in reality does not exist, and cannot exist, in God's Creation. It is only a representation, which they have created themselves, because they do not understand. Because this is their choice, they will get their wish, and I have to help them with this. They will see a real Satan, and they will experience things they wish to see, but it will not go as they expect, because they have to learn that they cannot rely on such forces. I will deliver what they wish to see, but they will lose control of it, and it will destroy them. Through sorrow and despair they will learn that their choice has no value."

We returned to the hall, and I had many question about the so-called fallen angels, and the story of Creation.

Nathaniel said, "The story of Creation tells you exactly what I have just demonstrated. Man had a choice. He was given the opportunity to make that choice. This was not the original sin, which you learned of when you were young. You have now learned that on different levels there are beings who are in between a normal soul and God. These beings have also had their choices in the past, and many chose the path of darkness. I am not responsible for them; another power greater than me is providing them with assistance. These beings who did fall into the darkness are for the most part on their way back to the light. They have become real angels of light. Sadly there are some who still dwell in the darkness, and they have nothing to do with Earth."

Nathaniel showed me some more examples and I understood the vast lesson which humanity still had to learn.

He went on, "You have now reached the end of this journey and I am glad to have met you. Think about me sometimes after you go back, and know that through your light, the task can be made easier. I too look forward to complete harmony, and wish fulfillment. We will meet again in the future. I wish you every happiness for the future."

We bade our goodbyes and made the long journey to the normal spheres. It was in many ways a relief to be back.

The angel spoke, "What you have seen answers your questions. The areas of Hell do not really exist, but are a projection of those who wish for the existence of such places. Their activities on Earth will be maintained by constructing a fantasy place like Hell. To facilitate this, the Creator has sent a being to provide assistance, since this choice is their right. In other words, the so-called areas of Hell are a projection of men, built with divine energy, and with divine assistance. These areas of Hell can disappear, once the souls who made the choice to go along the path toward the light. Have you understood all this?"

I nodded since I had understood it completely.

9

Sexuality within the soul

I was taken by the angel who had accompanied me on many journeys, to a classroom, in which there were a number of objects normally used for teaching Physics, Chemistry, and Biology. Another angel was waiting for us. He smiled as I shook his hand.

The angel began to explain, "Since you have had many questions related to sexuality we will provide you with a lesson, the content of which almost no one understands, and, if they do, they often do not want to accept, but which has enormous consequences for every soul in the Neutral Zone.

"The material bodies as you know them have been created by the gods a long time ago to serve as vehicles for the soul during its life on a planet. How this took place will never be revealed, and the reason for this is clear. The physics of a planet (such as temperature, light, gravity, and natural resources) determine what is suitable for life on that planet. The most universal appearance of such a body is hominid, or humanoid, which means that within reason, most intelligent beings look similar to yourself. This body design provides a great many opportunities for experiences and lessons, but there are also other forms of life, which you would not recognize as such. You have met some of those life forms during your journeys.

"The bodies that you know on Earth are of two genders, male and female, for which the blueprint is made during the second stage of evolution. At the creation of those bodies, feelings were built in to provide sexual pleasure, and a primitive form of attraction. This resulted in a fast-growing population on Earth and other planets. It also explains how humans are not solitary: they need other people. The sexual forces create a situation for the soul to seek relationships. The soul would never do this of its own accord. These feelings are primitive. They are mainly chemical, and are caused by the activity of various hormones within the body along with other chemical processes. In the beginning it was not so important how and when, and most importantly, with whom one made love, since there are a large amount of contact possibilities for the simple soul. But once one becomes spiritually aware, it will become important that one controls this process in a more advanced way. Pay attention now and you will see something which no one else has seen."

The angel laid his hands over my eyes, and I could feel them change through the warmth. I could now see materially, as well as spiritually at the same time, and the angel showed me two people engaged in love-making. Their spiritual level was simple and low. They were not at all developed. I could also see both their spirit bodies and their souls, and I saw that there were various energies working within them. I could see, however, that those energies were weak and did not gel with one another.

The angel went on, "The energies which they create, as they make love, are only weak, and if they attract a soul who would want to be their child, the result would be a child similar to them, also with a simple soul. Only on rare occasions, as a special lesson, would a spiritually developed child be born to such parents. Looking at this couple you can see that their energies do not really blend, because they do not have real, developed feelings of true love for each other. Only lust and attraction, which they mistook for love."

I looked again, to see two other people making love, and this time the situation was clearly different. Both individuals had a highly developed soul, which was spiritually aware. It could be seen in the spirit body as an enormous energy glowing intensely. The energy levels were in much greater harmony, but not yet perfect.

The angel said, "As you can see, this time the whole thing is very different. The energies are now able to attract a soul that is spiritually developed and aware. Their love-making is not only determined by attraction, but by a real sense of true love for each other, and this can be seen by the fact that their energies are mixing together." The couple were not finished, and I noticed that their energies dissolved, although small residues remained in each other's body. It appeared as if they kept each other's energy for a while.

The angel continued, "What you observed is of great importance, since there are indeed residues of energy left behind in the soul. This is because the soul cannot express itself clearly on its own, and is more or less tied to the human body. This fact was known in history, and is the real reason behind celibacy, and many cults and religions, although it is now almost forgotten. Pay attention now."

I looked again and saw another couple making love. One of the couple was spiritually developed, but the other was not. This time the energy levels in both their bodies was very bizarre. The energy generated in the developed soul almost overwhelmed that of the other partner, who clearly enjoyed this explosion, but for the partner with the developed soul it was very different. The soul was very tired. Furthermore, the combination of energies became more bizarre. It had different colors, and there was nothing recognizable.

The angel went on, "There is little attraction between those two and most definitely no love. If a child was born out of this, it would have a strange soul, who would be an exception in either a positive or negative way. It is in this sense that we may understand the phrase 'the sons of heaven who took daughters of men.' A spiritually developed soul combined with an undeveloped soul represents this idea. You can also observe that the residues that remain are much larger and are damaging in the material body, in particular to the one with the spiritually developed soul. If this relationship was to continue, you would see that the person with the developed soul would grow weaker and die prematurely."

I looked again, and this time saw a couple who were each other's complement. They were each other's twin soul. This time there was a massive energy stream, completely mingled with each other. There was no recognizable difference. Their souls had become one, and there was complete harmony.

The angel said, "This is unique and does not happen often on Earth, but will have to be attained by every soul in the future. As you can see the energies are now harmonized and have grown. A soul that is attracted by this energy would be of the same level as the parents and would show the same love as they have for each other. This form of love is the highest that can be attained, and this is your goal, as well as the goal of everyone in the universe. As you can see there are no residues this time, because they are complete and cannot resist the other's energy."

I thought a long time about everything I had seen and understood and realized that sexuality was something different from what I had thought.

Next I received some personal lessons and insights that made a deep impression on me.

The angel continued, "As you have seen, there are many aspects to love. You can now perhaps see that it is not good to be sexually so free. Simple-minded people still do this; they think that having multiple partners is being free, but in reality a lot of damage is caused without them being aware of it. In many different spiritual cults, especially those that have just started on the spiritual path, sexuality is seen as freedom and an expression of the true self. It is thought that the more sexual relationships one has, the more problems are worked out, and thus the human becomes free. In reality the opposite occurs, because sexuality is not only physical, but also spiritual and has a different character.

"You can discard statements and teachings which encourage free sexual behavior. The energies that are generated during sexual contact are powerful, and have a lasting influence on the soul, and you must take much more care with them than at present you realize.

"You must be clear about this in your own mind, because it is possible to influence somebody at a distance. That is how powerful this energy is. If you experience a strong sensual feeling about someone, then it is often the case that this person thinks about you with a sexual thought. This does not need to be always someone who lives in a material body. It can be a soul who does not live here. There are many forms of attractions and temptations and you have experienced this. It is not always easy to understand why people are attracted to each other, but you can take it that while physical attraction plays a small part, the main part is spiritual. In other words, one can feel the energies of each other that represent sexuality, and this can cause lots of stress to people. Many people harbor the thought that these forces have something to do with karma, and this may be possible in some cases, but it is not always the case. It is not good to let yourself go in such a situation. Do you understand all this?"

I replied in the affirmative because I really did. I said goodbye to the angel and, together with my companion, went back to my body, having learned and understood much.

v i s i o n

Ezekiel and the four elements

I was led by the angel who had accompanied me on earlier journeys.

"For some time now you have been working on understanding the visions of Ezekiel, and have many questions about them," she said, "and you will now be given an explanation. You have been unable to solve the mystery, because it is impossible to do so without the elements that I am going to show you now. The visions of Ezekiel have intrigued many people. Some have tried to interpret them, and been wrong, while others were moving in the right direction. Watch carefully, and if you have any questions, then let me know."

We undertook a journey, and arrived in a landscape, which was not real, but a background for an actual valley at the foot of a small range of hills. The valley was barren, with only a tiny amount of vegetation, and a small stream flowed through it, before emptying into a lake. It was dark, and the whole scene looked wild and uncultivated.

The angel continued, "This is where Ezekiel, the prophet, experienced his now famous vision. Pay attention because you are being granted the opportunity to see the vision again."

I watched, looking at the landscape, and for a while I did not see anything. Suddenly I became aware of a white illuminated cloud. It was a typical cloud, and could have come from a cartoon. It was ball shaped and sharply defined. It did not look like anything I was familiar with, and most certainly was no spaceship, and certainly not like anything that I had sometimes seen in illustrations. The cloud approached us, and stopped right in front of me. Then it appeared to dissolve on one side, to reveal something visible within it.

I saw something alive, which I had not seen before, and which could easily be a being, but yet it was not. It was just a living mass, which appeared to have a shape, and yet was shapeless. Surrounding this entity there were other beings I recognized from a previous journey in the Kingdom of Heaven: a dragon, a chormon, a god, and a complete soul.

The living mass enquired, "Why did you want to see this vision?"

I replied that I was intrigued by this part in the Bible, questioning what the prophet actually saw, and what the real message could be. I explained that I thought long and hard about the visions, and their meanings, and also how it might be possible to translate the visions to others so that they could be understood. I explained further that I felt the same predicament in not being able to describe what I experienced.

There was silence for a short time, but suddenly the cloud began to move. It appeared like a whirling, boiling mass and began to illuminate.

The voice of the living mass said, "As you have already known for some time now, the vision and revelations are not what they seem. They are provided to show humanity the path to be followed, but this path is often different from what one hopes or expects. If you have an experience and receive lessons during the journey, they are meant to help you; they are not always for others. Many prophets, seers, and people who have experiences make the mistake that they do not apply the experience to themselves, but go directly to others and preach that this is the way to go. This may be so, but one has to learn the lesson first as well. So too with Ezekiel. The man had the gift to experience visions, which could provide understanding to himself and his fellow men. He did this with great dedication, but it was also meant for him personally. The images he beheld were intended only for him, within his understanding, but he used them to provide advice to other people.

"You have now seen this vision again with the same images as the prophet once saw. You recognize some parts in this as the four representatives from Heaven who assist and influence the Earth and life itself. You have met them in their natural surroundings during earlier journeys, but if you did not know this, you could not describe this vision any more than Ezekiel could. This means that you have evolved and grown, and so can recognize the images you saw. But can you now also tell me if you have understood this vision?"

I thought a while, and then explained what sense the vision made to me. The cloud showed patterns and scenes, which were impossible to describe but which, when combined, gave a message of divine love and hope that men on Earth should have no fear about what was on the path ahead. The message also revealed that death should not be feared, and that physical death freed the spirit from a life that had run its course in its current form. It made clear that the spirit and souls, which were more or less imprisoned on Earth, should not despair, but in fact should see this imprisonment as a gift of the Creator to assist the soul, which is the only real part of men, to behold the light of Heaven. Without this experience, which is often painful, the soul cannot evolve.

The voice replied, "You have understood it correctly, but there is more to it than that. You have seen the four elements which assist Earth and which represent life as you know it. There are more elements, but they have nothing to do with life on Earth, and are meant for other planets. The four elements; the dragon, the chormon, the god, ✳ and the undivided soul are all that comprise what Earth is, will be, and has been. This means that humanity will always be assisted by those forces that come from me. I will never abandon humanity, and will always provide what is needed at the right moment. This means that much teaching will be done, since all of humanity is on its evolutionary path. The prophet's task was to convey this to his people. Whether he was successful in this is not of importance for you. It was his task, and he tried to do it as best as he could. It would be different now, because humanity is not the same as it was thousands of years ago. You are different, and think differently. This means that the same message would now be given, but with a different vision. Do you have any questions?"

I indicated yes, and asked why Ezekiel saw the image as a man,

chormon – see P. 101

67

while I saw only the living mass.

The voice replied, "I do not have a shape because I am in everything and in all you know. You know this, and I do not need to explain it. I will appear in any form, to anyone who wants me, in the shape that is expected. This means that if a child calls on me in despair, it will see me as a friendly person with a long silver beard, only because that's the image the child has of me. Because of this I am recognizable, and the child will feel safe. Ezekiel saw something that looked like a man, since that is what I was for him. I do not need to assume any shape for you, so that's why you do not see me. The fact that men will see me as a man is part of their thinking. Humanity believes that he is created in my image, and this has influenced many ways of thinking. Humanity forgets, however, that the apple tree, the ant, the tiger, and the grain of sand are also created in my image. Everything is created in my image, and the Earth with all its inhabitants, humans, plants, and animals are only one planet of the many millions in this universe, and this universe is one of the many in the area that you know as the Neutral Zone. You may now continue, and remember I am always with you."

The cloud dissolved immediately, and disappeared without a sound. The angel who accompanied me stood with me, and we talked about what we had seen.

"You have now seen Ezekiel's vision, and as you can see, it is different from what you thought. The image was only a vehicle to explain to the prophet something he had to explain to others. It was also a lesson for himself. Many visions are like that, but not everyone understands this, and the images become elements in themselves. There was no spaceship or machine, but that does not mean to say that they did not exist. Throughout the ages you have always had contact with those from other dimensions or planets, but this vision was not one of them."

The landscape dissolved, and we went back.

The angel concluded, "Be careful, because the future will be difficult for you. You have a degree of knowledge already. Have no fear. I am always with you."

v i s i o n

The energies within

I was taken to a classroom where I had been before, and my companion told me that I would be given answers to a number of questions I had about the spirit body, and the energies within. Another angel I knew him from previous experiences would do the teaching, but before he began, my companion said, "As a child you noticed many colors around both living and seemingly dead matter, but you did not know what they were. Later you learned them to be the radiation of an energy form, invisible to most people, and connected to the spirit body of the object you observed. Spiritual teachers called this an aura.

"Throughout the ages there have been many schools of thought about the aura, and various philosophies used this energy form to describe certain things within the spirit body. It is possible to study this energy form if the material body has an illness, or is subject to stress, in order to diagnose the causes. Furthermore, many people thought that they could heal the aura, and the body, with all kinds of hocus pocus. Many cults have addressed themselves to this activity, particularly in India and the Far East. But the aura is something very few people have really understood. Consequently there have been many errors, and what you have learned is not really correct. This is not a major problem, because everyone learns over time, and in these matters too mankind has to follow the learning process. Openness to these thoughts should be encouraged, but should never be a purpose in itself. It is useless to focus on your body, since it is only a vehicle for the short time you are here on Earth, and which you will put aside when your time has come. Because you have asked questions you will be given an important lesson. Remember it well. Watch carefully and if you have any questions please just ask."

I now paid attention to the angel, and by a movement of his hands over my eyes, he made me see a human body as completely transparent. I could see right through it, just like an X-ray. I could see all the internal organs, which were themselves also slightly transparent, but there was something else as well, emanating light. This was the spirit body.

The angel explained, "What you now see is a typical example of the material body, and within it a spirit body. The spirit body is created by the soul to control the material body, since the eternal soul needs this spirit body to express itself within a material body. Do you understand this?"

I indicated that I did.

The angel continued, "To make a body alive, and let it live, there are several different energies required. The shape of the body, as well as the gender, is determined by the soul, which also controls the growth of the body, so that it can be used for its task on Earth. The soul, however, requires an instrument to do this, since it does not have a form, which you would be able to recognize on Earth. The soul therefore receives a spirit body during the second stage of evolution [see Visions 2 and 3], and this spirit body, which is part of you for a long time, is able to transmit the signals from the soul to the material body."

I watched the transparent body again, and saw that all kinds of signals ran from the soul through the illuminated spirit body to the material body. It was fascinating to watch. Every function was visible. Energy flowed to and from the organs, and various signals were translated into material processes. This could be something simple like lifting a hand and arm, but also something complicated, such as thought about a difficult subject. There were various crossing points within the body. They looked like busy traffic junctions since they were very active. They were a bit like spinning suns, and radiated a lot of light.

The angel spoke again, "Look carefully because now there will be some changes."

I noticed that the person whose body this was experienced emotional stress. This was visible within the spirit body. There were now different flows of energy in different parts of the body. Some parts needed more, while others required less energy. The person felt this in his stomach and heart area; in the spirit body I could see that those areas glowed with intense activity. The person became ill. The illness had visible patterns within the spirit body, and these centers glowed as a result of the intense activity.

The angel explained, "Everything a person experiences has a certain expression within the spirit body. The soul is the final element to react and this is felt through the body. If one is nervous, then one may feel this in the chest area just above the stomach. Fear too is expressed in this region. Other feelings have their own specific problem area, and when one experiences emotional stress, it will be felt in the corresponding area. This is visible in the energy that radiates from the body, and it is this energy that is generally called the aura. Within this aura junctions can be seen, which coincide with the junctions within the spirit body you saw earlier. These junctions are called chakras and many people value them. They believe that those charkas are connected with certain physical and emotional functions within the body, but that is not correct. The chakras are only what is visible within the aura, and are similar to what is present within the spirit body. If you look carefully you can see those chakras."

I looked again at the transparent body, and I indeed saw the aura as I had done when I was a child. Within this aura I saw the chakras at places corresponding to the energy junctions in the spirit body. The chakras, however, were only a dim expression of the real energy junction, as if a black piece of cloth had been placed over a torch. That was the difference in brightness between the chakras in the aura, and the real junctions within the spirit body.

The angel continued, "Many schools of thought hold that the chakras can be influenced by spiritual healing activities. They believe that by working with the chakras it is possible to heal the material body, and also lead a more emotionally balanced life. In reality this is not possible, because the visible chakras within the aura are only a reflection of the real junction points within the spirit body. Looking at the chakras can only tell you what is happening, but not the reason why it is happening. In other words one can use the chakras as a monitor, but the vibration within them is not the cause of the problem. It is therefore not possible to help a patient with a severe depression or trauma by giving him or her a spiritual healing session in the aura and the chakras, and then expect results. The healing must come from within the soul, which is very well aware of the real cause. Almost all illnesses of this type can be healed within, but only with self-honesty, since the soul always knows what is right, and what is wrong.

"Physical ailments cannot be healed either with spiritual healing, since most of them are a result of prolonged wrongdoing. This can be wrong food, or work with chemicals, or whatever, but the illness is only the outward expression of what the person has done wrong, often unawares. One can try to heal this with herbal remedies, and spiritual exercises, or by means of operations and heavy medicines, but it is often the case that the medical profession only looks at the illness in isolation. Consequently there is temporary relief, but the real cause is not being tackled. The real problems will therefore remain visible within the spirit body, and unless a person tackles his own mental or physical problems from within the soul, he will fall ill or become depressive again. Do you understand?"

I indicated that I had understood that it was not much use to follow certain meditations to tune in to the chakras or other things, if one did not understand the real function of the spirit body and its energy. I had a question, which rose out of a documentary I had seen, in which it was claimed that by applying electrical stimuli to the brain, and in particular the temporal lobes, certain paranormal appearances could be created such as the vision of a spirit, near-death experiences, and other less well-documented experiences. The researcher in this area stated that all experiences were only the product of the brain itself, which could be re-created at will in a lab.

The angel smiled and said, "That doctor has done well to have found that out. It is correct that if you stimulate something, you will get a reaction. The brain, however, is the translator between the soul and the material body through the spirit body. Without well-functioning brains the soul cannot express itself within the body, which is its temporary home. What the researcher does not realize is that the brain in itself is only a mass of proteins and carbon compounds, water and blood. It is only an organ. Granted it is a special organ, but it remains an organ, which does not have any life in itself, no knowledge and no information, and will return to dust once the body dies. It is the soul that provides the real information. The reason that the researcher reached those conclusions is that most people leave their bodies during their sleep, or have dreams where they have many experiences that would be called paranormal in their waking state. The vast majority of people are not aware of this. Yet it does take place, since without these experiences mankind would be unable to live and learn, since every step is guided. In other words, the experiences have already taken place, and are stored in the brains. Through stimulation it is possible to re-live the experiences, but these experiences do not take place at that moment in time. The experience has already occurred, and is only consciously remembered.

"Another situation is that the state of the brain is temporarily altered as a result of stimulation. It becomes more sensitive, and can experience on a wider range. Consequently a paranormal experience can indeed take place. However, for people who don't believe such things, it appears that the stimulation is the only cause. Chemical substances can do this as well as certain drugs. Please ignore the information you saw on television, because there is not much value in it. Only at the time when mankind wants to research this, and can understand the soul and accept it for what it really is, can real discoveries be made."

I understood this explanation, and that the lesson was over, but the angel held me back for a moment and said, "It is important that you learn this lesson well, because you will have strange experiences, and encounter strange things. You will need this knowledge then, and if you have questions, call me because I am always there."

I thanked the angel, and after a long journey with my companion, I was back in my body.

The angel of life

I left my body and was taken by the angel who had accompanied me before on many journeys. Being with this angel was so familiar that I felt at ease, and completely able to trust. It came naturally to me to enquire what the purpose of this journey would be.

She smiled and said, "You will see this soon enough. This time it is my task to lead you to a teacher who will show you something you need to know."

We continued on our way, until we arrived in a landscape, which defied any description. After a while we reached a hilltop, on which was a strange building. Close to the building there stood a being dressed in white. As I drew nearer, I noticed that this being had a grand countenance. She created a strange impression. She stood holding a wand vertically.

I thought, "This is the Angel of Death." She must have guessed my thoughts, since a faint smile became visible.

She spoke, "I am who I am, and I cannot give you my name yet. Only when you have left your mortal coil will you be permitted to know this. I am the Angel of Life, since death does not exist in God's Creation. What men call death is only transformation to a new life and new level of consciousness. I will show you a great lesson. Watch carefully since your own future, and that of humanity, will depend on this. If you have any questions then let me know immediately."

The angel looked up to the sky, and held up her wand. The clouds parted and an enormous vision was visible. The images were all around us, and it appeared as if we were inside the images. I saw images of Earth and its history. Most of this was known to me from earlier journeys and lessons, but there was something there that I had not seen before. It appeared to be sharper, and I could see the individual lives of each person on Earth. This was rather confusing since there were so many, and it was almost impossible to concentrate on one person. Yet somehow it was possible to see every soul within one image. I could see the past, the present, and the future path. It was visible as a kind of faintly illuminated thread, on which there were various points of importance to the soul.

It was clear that the Angel of Life was very influential in the lives of every human being. It was also evident that the end of the physical life, the death of the material body, was determined by her. This could be seen as a small flash of light in the life path of the soul. Each time that small flash of light was visible was the point when that person died, and his or her soul undertook the journey to the spheres. The intensity and the colors of the light flash determined the method and the reason for death. This could not be described in earthly words but somehow the light and the color conveyed the whole message.

It was an enormous sight since there were billions of those threads with many flashes. Other images showed other important moments in the life of a person.

The Angel of Life continued, "Pay attention now. Then you can see something which is very important."

I looked toward the area she pointed toward, and noticed that some threads joined for a while, and then separated again. The angel said, "These are the human relationships; this can be a love relationship but also a business, or a hate relationship. Nature does not matter all that much, but here you can see how and why many people have relationships with each other."

I looked further, and realized that some threads seemed to join, and suddenly flash. The individual flashes of light of those who died together on Earth were visible as a larger flash of light, and I noticed that there were quite a few of those larger flashes.

The angel continued, "What you see now is a representation of what you can recognize on Earth as a disaster. That large flash over there was the event you know on Earth as the disaster in New York where many thousands died. Other larger flashes of light represent an air disaster, an epidemic, or a war."

I was deeply impressed and the angel now pointed to the area still in front of us.

I looked at all the threads, and noticed that the number of large flashes increased in number and intensity. It appeared that the near future held many events during which many people would leave their material body. I looked further, and then suddenly I noticed a massive explosion of light, which seemed to be connected to all the threads. Then everything was dark. I was rather shocked by what I had seen, and asked the angel the meaning of this event.

She had a serious expression on her face and said, "That is the physical end of the planet Earth. Do you understand this?"

I indicated that I did, and was silent for a while. I did not think that this event was so close, and never thought for a moment that the way this would happen would be so strange.

"Do not worry about something which has nothing to do with you. The end of the Earth is part of its Creation, and as you know it is not unique. There are millions of planets like the Earth within God's Creation and Earth is only one of them. There have been many disasters that have wiped out life on Earth, and yet there is always a new seed that will grow. All will start again. What you have seen this time is that the material end of the Earth is not a punishment from God. God will not do that. You do this yourself. There won't be a soul who can ever blame God for the end of Earth, and what will happen to mankind. Whatever happens mankind causes. This is something you know already, so remember it well."

The image began to change now, and new things became visible. I could see deeper into certain situations, as well as details of individuals or small groups of people. I could see the many events that had to be experienced by mankind. Most of them could be easily understood. There were happy events and sad events, but everything was designed in such a way that a lesson was given to those who needed to experience it.

I could now see my own thread, or life path, as well as those of other people I knew, and was surprised to see that those threads did not go into the large fireball.

The angel explained, "That is because your fate, as well as that of some others, is not connected with the fate of Earth and humanity. You have to accomplish a task that is of the greatest importance. You will receive a lot of help since you cannot do this alone. With you there will be many others both in spirit and in the material world who will help. It is your task to ensure that the threads that you could not see after the large fire flash will be visible again, and to provide them with a new future. Watch carefully."

I looked again toward the strange scene and discovered that the threads behind the large flash of light had not disappeared, but had been re-routed to a different sphere. They had changed. It was not possible to describe this in words, but it looked like an enormous colorful energy game with sparks, whirls, and a lot of light in the most wonderful colors. There were billions of light points, which had been threads, and each of those light points represented a divine soul that had hitherto lived in a human body. The color game became more intense, and at a certain moment metamorphosed into one sea of light, which was purple-blue in color. The sphere opened and I could see that new threads were created. It was the beginning of a new creation. Very slowly, one by one, I saw new threads emerge from the sphere. They increased in numbers, until a certain point was reached when there were just as many as before the big flash of light had ended their existence.

But something strange had occurred. The threads appeared more radiant, and cleaner. They were clearly the same threads, but had obviously passed through a process of cleansing and improvement. I could now follow their paths again, and watched them become m ankind of the future. The colors of the scene spoke a different language now. They had become aware and had learned a lot.

My companion said, "As you have seen, life goes on. There will be no end to God's Creation but the material forms as you know them now will change. This means that on a material level many things will disappear, and one of those is the Earth and its inhabitants. They will live on in spirit, and undergo a process of increased awareness. You have been able to see this in the sphere you saw. When all is ready the seed will be planted in the new world and it will grow. New bodies will be born, and new worlds will be created. Everything will then start again, but in an improved form. Humanity will be given the opportunity to discover new things that are not possible in your present society and way of life. The capacity of the brain and the thought processes will be increased tenfold and new levels of consciousness will be revealed, which are closed at the present time. Mankind will also learn to discover the divine source in everything and to accept this. This is God's promise, and it is up to you to plant this seed, which will make everything possible."

I was silent and thought things over. I had many questions but the angel spoke again.

"I know you have many questions, but it is not good to know everything just yet, since you have to grow toward certain things. You must have some experiences before you reach complete understanding. I am always with you, even though you won't see me as you have been allowed to do just now. I will answer all your questions at the right time. Nothing will remain misunderstood. Remember that all answers come when they are needed. You will now return to your material home, and you will receive what is needed. I will send what is required and remember: all is in God's hands and I fulfill His wish."

I said goodbye to the Angel of Life, and shook hands. I felt a warmth that I had never previously felt. I was deeply impressed. My companion was there, and took me by the hand. Together we went to the place where I lived. I was very quiet, thinking about what I had seen.

My companion gently broke the silence.

"I hope you can see and understand that what you experience on Earth at the moment is not quite what it appears to be. Be thankful that you are freed from a situation which had a grip on you in the old world, which is a world no more in the eyes of God."

I could understand this and after a long discussion on matters of a personal nature I returned home.

13

The nine dimensions of life

I was taken to a Physics classroom. The room was empty of people, but contained models used for demonstrating the laws of Physics. In the center of the room was a Being of Light — we might call her an angel — who began to explain these laws in a very simple manner. She picked up a little stick and indicated that we were in the first dimension. I was not impressed, since this was knowledge I had learned in school. She smiled, however, and, disregarding my impatience, went on to explain three-dimensional mathematics. To do so, she constructed a cube, empty inside, a skeleton made from twelve sticks and eight joints.

She then picked up a brick. This was solid, made from very small particles of sand, cement, and clay. Indicating the brick, the angel said, "You can see that it is far more complicated than you think if you really wish to describe a three-dimensional space. All these tiny particles are part of this stone, and an apparently solid body must therefore be described differently from the simple X, Y, and Z coordinates, which I used with the sticks."

She placed the stone on a white table.

"Watch carefully. I will push the stone to the other side of the table to show you that, when you want to describe an object, you also have to state, not only its three-dimensional properties, but also WHEN this object was. In the original position, at this moment, there is nothing left. However, the brick is now visible in a new position. This is the new dimension, which you may, for the moment, call the fourth dimension."

I understood this, but wondered what she was inferring through the doubt raised by the phrase "for the moment."

Again she smiled and said, "If you look at the surface of the table, you will see that during the pushing of the brick to the other side, small particles of the brick were loosened and are now on the table."

I did so and saw sand, dust, and grime on the previously white table surface.

The angel continued, "This means that during the move from one position to the other, the brick has changed. In other words the brick is no longer what it was at the beginning of the process. Small particles have broken off as the result of the process of movement. Change has taken place. If you can now see all material objects on Earth, or indeed in the universe, from a three-dimensional point of view, as mankind normally does, then you will discover that nothing remains the same with the passing of time. Everything changes. There is wear and tear. Things grow older. Many types of change take place. Even if this brick had remained in its original position, change would have occurred. The brick would have absorbed water from the atmosphere, altering its composition. Even its mechanical properties would have been affected. From this it is clear that the fourth dimension is somewhat more complicated than simply "when" an object is in situ. Do you understand this?"

I remained silent and the angel continued, "Time as a dimension is something you cannot really comprehend, because you do not know all the factors that influence life. I named this dimension the fourth 'for the time being,' because in reality this mechanism is very complicated, and is a combination of many physical laws. We will return to this so-called fourth dimension once we have completed the journey I will take you on, the purpose of which is to show you all the other dimensions. You will then know and understand the truth of the reality. It is now time to leave this classroom, and begin our journey. Watch carefully and if there is something you do not understand, please say so. I am here to help you."

We went into "space." There the light was filtered with many colors and stars and nebulae. Amidst this was a second bright being (again we might call her an angel), who explained the building blocks of Creation. She held out the atom carbon and, with a movement of her hands, took apart, piece by piece, the electrons, protons, and neutrons of the atom and put them in three little boxes. She picked up other atoms, hydrogen and uranium, and did the same with them. The three boxes were now filled with neutrons, protons, and electrons, and it was no longer possible to determine from which atom they originated. Next she selected from each box a single particle and, with a movement of her hands, she pulled six smaller particles from the proton, four particles from the neutron, and two particles from the electron. They resembled what we would recognize as the suits of hearts or spades. They vibrated and radiated a tremendous sense of fun. They were alive and engrossed in playing together.

The particles were not identical. They each had their own constituents to determine the properties of the electron, neutron, and proton. Next the angel took these particles and separated them, and I realized that each particle consisted of eighteen smaller particles, all identical. The angel explained that all matter was made out of this single particle. At first glance it looked like a tiny sphere, but, on close examination, I saw that this was not the case. It was a point of light, energy, and matter, and took many forms. At the same time the angel explained that, depending on the will of God, this piece of light, or quantum divine energy, as it could be called, could take the properties from which not only protons, neutrons and electrons, but also antimatter and particles like muons for instance, could be formed. But this was not all. The particle also had the potential for completely different properties, and thus was able to create situations and scenes, which could be called spiritual rather than material. It was also possible, she said, to make material forms completely unknown to us, which did not use neutrons, protons, and electrons. In other words this divine piece of light or energy had all the possibilities of the universe contained within it. The spiritual, as well as the material, was also built from the same particle.

The angel explained that there was no difference between the spiritual and material world. It is only the perception of mankind that distinguishes them. For God everything is a possibility of expression. Next the angel showed me a "family tree" on a large screen. On top I saw the divine particle and beneath there were many different systems derived from it, each of which led to different, and to us unknown, revelations. I recognized our system amidst those unfamiliar to me. I saw clearly how atoms were built from the divine particle, and formed into the elements we know. I also saw into the spiritual non-material world.

The angel continued, "As you can see, the system in which you live and work is built from a specific family of elements, which all come from the same source. This is governed by a dimension, which, for the moment, you may call the fifth. This dimension ensures that all these systems are not colliding with each other, and that every system, both material and spiritual, is neatly separated from its fellows as far as is necessary.

"This dimension is the smallest expression of the Divine and contains everything. The will of the Creator determines which property in the particle, or divine energy, is used, and also what will be manifest. This difference in properties, which is determined by God, is the new dimension."

I had no difficulty in understanding this and, in a single moment, many mysteries on Earth had an explanation.

We continued our journey and, while this was still the same space, we were now at a different spot and I saw a new picture. The angel showed me a scene very familiar on Earth. It was a street in a city filled with people and cars. Children walked and played on the street.

The angel spoke, "Tell me what you see." I told her what I saw; this was straightforward because it all looked solid and real. "Watch now carefully because I will change something."

The angel moved an object, and suddenly a different scene appeared. There was now a landscape, but this time with human beings busy with the harvest. It appeared almost like a TV scene where the angel could change the channels.

The angel explained, "Both scenes are real, and are in the same space, but they are separated because the wavelength and frequencies from both material groups are not identical. Do you understand this?"

I said yes, because this was just like radio waves, which are separated by different wavelengths and frequencies. This is the principle on which it is possible for us to receive many different radio and TV broadcasts, without them disturbing each other.

"Watch now carefully and I will show you the first scene again."

Once again I saw the street, and then the angel moved another object. The image began to disappear. It fragmented into small points held together by some form of energy. It was still possible to recognize the street scene, but only with great difficulty.

The angel said, "This is reality for us. What you saw a moment ago, as real and solid objects, is only a collection of atoms and particles held together by a signal, or energy, to create an image, which you translate into a scene. The signal, which arranges the atoms, and therefore arranges the street scene, is more important than the objects themselves, since this signal always has the power to create such images. It is even possible to repeat the signal at any point, and thereby recreate the scenes. The physical form is only the expression of the signal, which is given by God. Do you understand this?"

I said yes because it made sense to me. I looked again toward the scene, wondering about the enormous amount of empty space, which is in all living and material objects. It appeared an inefficient use of space. The angel smiled, however, and yet again moved an object. The street scene and the landscape were now both visible as little points, which were separate signals, and yet at the same time, the images overlaid one another. They both inhabited the same space, but they did not interact with each other, because the signal that created the images had different frequencies and wavelengths. The angel explained that these frequency variations could be seen as a new form of housekeeping dimension. This dimension ensured that every form built by the divine Creator could neatly and orderly co-exist. The angel said that in reality many thousands of worlds occupied the same space, and that this was also the case with our own world. The world as we know it is unique, and what we experience as reality is only one of the many channels or programs possible in the space we occupy.

I gazed toward the endless space, and I wondered why so many images had to be compressed into so small an area in this space. The universe appeared to be large enough, and there were so many empty planets and stars, as well as gaps between them. The angel smiled again, and with one movement showed me every creation in existence, on every possible frequency in the universe. Everything was suddenly a sea of light. Billions of color variations, most of which I did not know and had never seen before, became visible. Billions of stars and planets and nebulae, along with other objects I did not recognize, were basking in a divine glow of a strange but incredibly beautiful light. Literally every corner of the universe became a sea of light and activity. Not a fragment or corner of space was empty. The emptiness was filled with activity, visible in a multiplicity of frequencies.

Many of the scenes would be difficult to describe. I was aware that what was happening was completely unknown to me, and divine in origin. I looked a long time at this, searching for Earth, but I could not find it, because it was too small. The angel helped me and enlarged the small world where mankind lives. It was tiny and I felt small and strange.

Was this all the world really was? The angel spoke, "Yes, that is all, and yet it is not insignificant, because you must remember that all you see is in harmony with everything else. Or rather that is how it should be. You know that this is not the case, and that it is the task and duty of all of us to restore this harmony and let it grow. The world you know on Earth is only one of these worlds, and only a small one, but just as important as any other note in a musical harmony. It cannot be belittled or ignored. The space you see, which appears vast for you, is only one of the many universes, which are all brought together in the Neutral Zone. The existence of the Neutral Zone has already been explained to you on your previous journeys, and you saw how this functions the first time you were in the absolute reality of Heaven. It is not as it is viewed by mankind and their spiritual teachers." (See Visions 2 and 3.)

The angel restored the image to its original state and everything appeared to be again as it was before. There was a wonderful calm.

The angel spoke again saying, "This is the sixth dimension and its role is to keep everything neatly in order so God's Creation is separated in an orderly way."

Following this the angel led me again to another section of the same space, for a further lesson. The street scene of before was again visible, crowded with many people. They looked like humans in as much as they had arms, legs, a body, and a head, and there was the familiar variety of appearance and beauty. The angel laid her hands over my eyes, and through their warmth I could feel that my eyes were changed. She removed her hands, and I looked again toward the people in the street. But everything was different now. I could no longer recognize them as people. Only their real selves, their souls, could be seen.

The angel spoke again, "In the spiritual lessons you have learned that every soul is on its way toward the light of God. But, as you know, the process is not the same for every soul. Some souls learn the lessons quickly, while others are slow. They prefer their daily life in the material world and enjoy themselves. What you are looking at now is the spiritual reality of each soul. You can see that each soul has its own level of awareness indicated on a frequency. You may view this as a form of energy level. The souls, which are advanced in their journey, have a higher energy level than the ones still far away from the Light."

It was not a pleasant sight because many souls looked fearful and grotesque.

The angel said, "You know very well that every soul is on its way and that it will return to God in time. Do not worry about this. The spiritual frequency, or energy level, of a soul at any given point, provides an indication of the position of the soul on its path toward God. You may call this the seventh dimension."

We then set out on a long journey through "space," during which we discussed many things. We arrived at a place that I recognized as the Neutral Zone, where souls come from the Kingdom of Heaven to be grouped in a variety of evolutionary waves. Once the soul has entered one of these evolutionary states it cannot change it, and the path has to be followed until the journey to the Light has been completed. I knew all this, as I had been allowed to travel many times in this area, and I understood what the angel meant.

"Once the souls are here, they are divided into groups, and sent on a specific evolutionary path which has been chosen for them," she continued. "This situation may be called the eighth dimension, and it determines which path has to be followed by the soul. There are many paths available. Come and I will show you what you have already encountered during your previous journeys into the real Heaven, but which at that point you were not permitted to have true knowledge of."

We climbed a "mountain" (not a real mountain but the experience felt like one), and I could see the vastness of the entire Neutral Zone. I saw a variety of universes filled with billions of stars, planets, and nebulae. Everywhere was alive and humming. There was no empty space. It was not possible from this point to see any details because everything was so vast. I stood and watched in amazement, and far, far away I could see the translucent and bright borderline, which was the real border between the Neutral Zone and the true Kingdom of Heaven. I recognized this as I had seen it on earlier journeys but from the other side, that is from the Kingdom of Heaven, looking toward the Neutral Zone.

Suddenly I was aware that a strange, glowing darkness had appeared from a corner and looked as if it was moving toward us. It was not black, but had a purple color streaked with dark red and dark blue.

The angel spoke, "What you see now is not real darkness, and it does not come any closer. It is not a threat and despite your feeling toward it, it is most certainly not a negative force. What you are looking at has been made visible for you by God, out of love for you, and is the area of the anti-force. Imagine that all you see now has its complete opposite in the anti-system. This system has nothing directly to do with us, but is very important. Both systems keep each other in balance. On earlier journeys you have seen a small part of this anti-force, and you have seen how this mechanism functions. You have been able to see how this works to provide the souls with awareness, and how the soul is separated from the Kingdom of Heaven. This is what is known to Christians as the Fall of Man, but you know differently. We have told you that the Neutral Zone is the area where the soul can grow and learn, but the anti-force is much bigger than you can imagine. It is not good to have too much knowledge about this force at this point in your learning, as it is very complicated."

The angel was silent and she too looked for a long time toward the anti-forces and the anti-field.

She continued, "The anti-forces keep the gods in balance, and together they form the real God. You have already seen a great deal, but it is better that we do not go any further for the moment. As you can see, it is possible for the soul to belong to that system, and you may view this as the last and the ninth dimension. It determines if a manifestation belongs to this, or to the anti-system."

Within seconds we were back in the classroom and the angel said, "In short you have now seen the nine dimensions, which you need to describe anything within the Neutral Zone. You can now describe the shape of an object, and also when this object is there. You can find the divine origins, and determine to which material or spiritual group a soul belongs. You have seen the housekeeping functions, and also the spiritual energy level. Finally you have seen the various evolutionary possibilities, and the potential of the anti-forces. Beyond these nine dimensions there are no others essential for describing any form of life, but there are many so-called help functions. Sometimes it is necessary that, in order to teach a particular lesson, a situation, temporary or permanent, is created to suit certain conditions. Help functions can provide these changes, but it is not possible to call these real dimensions, although they may be experienced by people in this way. There are many variations possible to these help functions. But for now we will continue with the most difficult, but also the most important, part of the lesson. In the beginning I referred to the so-called fourth dimension and I told you that you may call it the fourth, for the time being. This dimension is very strange, and I will explain why this is so."

The angel took me to a space, in which a strange landscape was visible. It seemed very unnatural, but yet it had a beauty, which was very unusual. It was a kind of desert, with strange mountains and strange lakes. The colors also were alien to me and, although many people would find this place fearful, I felt fully at ease, and I was glad that I had been allowed to see it. This was strange, since I had never been there, and yet I felt that I "knew" this place, and that it was a place of happiness.

In front of me was a scene, not easy to describe, but to me it was Life. This is difficult to imagine since there was no familiarity in the images, but the whole scene encapsulated life in all its aspects. A human being, a typical nuclear reaction, a chemical process, a burning candle, the birth of a star, and the evolution of the soul were only a few of the images I could see. The whole place was alive. It moved, humming with activity. It grew and there was light.

The angel said, "What you see now is an image of all that is alive in the fullest possible way that men can understand. As you can see, everything is alive and moving. The process of life changes things, and from God's point of view, these changes are a form of evolution or growth. The nuclear reaction will split the atom, and there is radiation. The human being grows and becomes old. The star will go through its stages and become a red giant, before it implodes and dies. The candle will burn itself out, and the chemical reaction brings about changes in matter. These are all processes that take time. Mankind has tried to understand this time factor in order to explain its force. It has often been called the fourth dimension, and I too have done this at the beginning of this exercise. The truth is somewhat different, and I am now going to teach you a lesson of great importance. I know that you wrestle with the problem of time in your daily life, so watch carefully and, if there is something you do not understand, please ask because I am here to help you."

The angel moved an object and the moving, living scene before my eyes stood still. Everything was more or less frozen in time. The angel had stopped time. I looked very carefully, and saw that the human beings did not move. Nor did they grow older. The nuclear reaction was frozen, and the particles stood still in their position. The stars also stood still, as did the chemical reaction. The candle ceased to burn, and the flame was not visible.

The angel said, "You see how life can be stopped because time is something different from the process which humans experience. You have observed this in other lessons and tasks, but you will see now what the process, wrongly called time, really is." I looked intently toward the frozen scene. At the same time I also watched outside it. Everything continued there just as it had before. The figures changed and grew older, but the forms inside the scene did not.

The angel spoke, "If we leave this situation like this, then it will stay unaltered forever. The changes have stopped and no time will pass. Change, for instance the human body growing older, has nothing to do with the processes, which men think they understand. It is the process, which you call time, which causes the changes. These changes are expressed as wear and tear, chemical and other processes. Through this misunderstanding humans have failed to grasp divine law. It is of the greatest importance that you stop using the word 'time,' since you are using it inaccurately, and thus creating problems. It is better to see this process as an energy form, or the driving force of all the processes of life, both material and spiritual. As you can see, without this driving force everything stops, and no change takes place. The speed of the process, time, depends on all the other dimensions which I have shown you, and is determined by God. Even on Earth this may differ for each object and each human being. You may think that a week has passed on the calendar if you have had seven days with twenty-four hours, but this is not the case. The real processes of time are very complicated and, depending on your spiritual awareness, it is even possible to escape this process.

"Furthermore, these processes are different at each point in the Neutral Zone. A soon as you leave the atmosphere of the Earth you will encounter them differently. The duration of time in the Neutral Zone is not the same throughout. Consequently it is not possible to determine the correct age of the solar system or the universe. Scientific data on the universe has been invented by mankind, and are not real. The real process is a divine energy, which provides the opportunity to reach your goal. This process varies its influence and speed depending on whether or not you are directly on course toward this goal, or if, by your own failings, you are distracted from it. This is the real process of change, and it takes place on many possible levels as you have seen. Not a single process, not even a nuclear reaction, can take place without this driving divine energy, which pushes all ahead. Without it everything would be lifeless.

"Yet, this is still not the complete picture, because you have also seen the anti-forces. The processes, which I just described, and which are complicated enough, have their opposites. It is difficult to comprehend this but it can be observed."

I was silent and pondered a long time on everything she had said.

I could understand the lesson. It made sense as long as I was in this landscape, but I wondered if I would still comprehend it once I was back home.

The angel smiled and said, "Have no fear because you will be able to understand. Watch carefully and I will show you a simple example."

I saw a human body on the molecular level. I watched cell division. The cells renewed themselves according to a perfect pattern, and depending on where, and which cells, and their function in the bodies, the renewal process took place at a tremendous speed. Some cells were not older then a year, while the oldest were about seven years.

The angel went on, "As you can see, the body in this example is never older than seven years. Purely from a chemical and biological point of view this body is never more than seven years of age. Yet this being is seventy years old, and the body will show this, while biologically there is no reason to do so. Age and ageing is therefore somewhat different from the biological way of growing older of the building blocks of the body. The signal, or programming or pattern of the body, is what causes the changes, and this expresses itself in all the known processes, which you can read in any good medical book. It is this that makes you grow older. Control of the signal or pattern would make possible control of the processes in the body. Something similar takes place on a planetary level, and also in the entire universe. Everything changes, but is also renewing itself. On a level you would not be able to recognize, your planet is currently being renewed. So also is the whole universe. Yet you still look for age and ageing. Just as in the previous example, you will calculate that the body is seventy years old, while the building blocks are not more than seven years. On a larger scale this is the same. The many changes, which have occurred during evolution, are such that you cannot and need not search for age. Everything, even the hardest stone, is subject to this type of change and renewing. Maybe you can see now that time, duration of time, and processes of time must be viewed in a different way. What you will notice is only the result of something you do not understand, but is not in itself the cause of certain processes. The things you have seen are only the expression of the phenomenon, the divine driving force, but do not in themselves exist. Since every manifestation of God's Creation is different and unique, the divine driving forces of these processes of time are also unique for each of these manifestations. It is therefore impossible to think logically about time (present, past, and future), since each manifestation experiences its own processes. What for one person is future is already the past for someone else. This fourth dimension can be analyzed in many different ways, since it depends on a plethora of situations and dimensions. You yourself determine the influence and measure of this divine driving force by the way you live, work, and think. It is therefore not good to live your life, your work, and your thinking being determined by this process, while in reality you yourself determine it. Take stock and take control over yourself; you will then find that the demands of time imposed by others, and your surroundings, no longer control you. You are then free and have created a direct link with God."

I was silent because I understood the teaching. I did not have any questions at that point, but I knew that I would in the future.

The angel smiled and said, "Come, we will go back home. You have seen a great deal, and learned a great deal. Now it is time for action. On your next journey we will enter the field of the anti-forces".

Vision

14

The Kingdom of Heaven

I was taken to infinity by a very beautiful angel. Before we set out she said, "You will now take a journey through the known universe. Pay attention because you will see many new things."

As I "floated" through the vast space of the universe, I realized that it was not black like the night sky. There was a myriad of colors, clouds, stars, and nebulae, alive and vibrating.

"This is your life system, and contains on different levels, all the spiritual areas where humans go once they have shed their earthly body," my guide said. "Everything takes place here. What you are looking at, however, is not the completed absolute. We will go on to infinity where you will see that the real Heaven is somewhat different from what humanity believes. Heaven has been created in men's minds, but it has been born out of their fear and desire. Consequently man's picture is not true. Many images at the spiritual level seen by men are taken as real, and are experienced as such, but they are only a creation of man's thinking. This inaccurate picture of Heaven has been damaging. Many religions and spiritual teachings, which invest in this inaccuracy, can unintentionally stop spiritual growth. They can do more harm than good. But the thoughts of the souls of men are very powerful, and can create images and shapes, which are true to their spiritual homes. This is not always obvious to you, and you must learn to distinguish between what is real and from God's source, and what has been invented by man. Watch carefully

95

and I will show you something."

The angel put her hands over my eyes, and through the warmth of her hands, my eyes changed, and I was able to see "spiritually." Strange scenes appeared in front of me: what seemed to be little islands, which were very beautiful and of varied shape and landscape. On these islands lived spirits and souls, their position dependent on the level and position of the island. Each soul was working hard to go to the next, the higher island.

The angel explained, "What you see now are the spiritual habitats, where the souls live and work, once they no longer live in their material bodies. As you can see, life and work goes on, but in a different form. These places are created by men with help from the spiritual teachers and divine helpers, but it is not Heaven. The appearance of these islands is very limited. It is dependent on background, culture, and race. Watch carefully. Man lives his life in such a way that he makes no room for different races or creatures from other planets. Can you now see how this works? All processes of life, both in the material world and in the spiritual world, are an integral part of the evolutionary route, and it ceases once humanity can understand the reality of Heaven. This is God's plan. All spiritual habitats and levels are given with love from God in order to teach men. But they have to learn that it can never be a purpose on its own. If someone on Earth feels down and sad, and is hungry, then he or she will want to leave that life, and wish for a better place. But this may never be one's goal. The journey is just as important as the final destination, which for most part is unknown to mankind.

"It should be equally clear that there is no such thing as dying or eternal sleep.

"Life is everlasting and does not stop. The soul will live forever and will always have to work. Physical death is only the passing to a new phase, where other lessons will have to be experienced and learned. Do you understand all this?"

I did so. It was very clear to me. I thought of the many religions and spiritual teachings that describe Heaven. If humanity could really comprehend this, it should be obvious that these descriptions were too limited, and that this meant that there really is something beyond.

The angel went on, "We will now leave here and continue, because your journey has not yet ended."

We floated again on our way. After a considerable time, during which we encountered endless masses of stars, planets, and spiral nebulae, it appeared that the surroundings were darker and more empty then before. The angel said, "We are now reaching the border of the known universe, and in a few moments, we will pass it. Watch very carefully, because this is very important."

We flew for a short while and arrived at a thin see-through wall, which felt like a form of jelly. We went through this, and an entirely new scene appeared before my eyes. I looked in wonder. The universe, which we had now left behind, appeared to be packed in a separate sphere of jelly. The surroundings were very different now, and other similar spheres were visible, moving slowly in a strange light. I had seen on earlier journeys that small groups of star systems seemed to be packed in similar spheres. Within the universe there were always twelve star systems connected to each other in this way, and all of them with a shell around them. All these shells moved in a particular fashion and direction, but only now could I see that the entire universe was also in one of those shells. We continued the journey and from the position that we were now in, it was possible to see many spheres or shells each containing a complete universe. Each universe consisted of many star systems, divided into groups of twelve. Each group was also wrapped in an invisible shell, which floated through the universe.

"What you see now is the space of the Neutral Zone. This space, which is filled with many universes, as you are now aware, is limited and has borders. It is only one of the many areas within the true reality or Kingdom of Heaven. We are now near the border of the Neutral Zone, but your journey and your lessons are not yet complete. I cannot continue with you, but other beings will do so, and they will teach you. I will wait here until your journey through the heavens has been completed, and then take you back to Earth."

I bade goodbye to my companion, and went over the border of the Neutral Zone to a place I had no words to describe. There, there were a number of beings, unlike anything I had ever seen before. Their voices sounded in my head, but with no familiar form of telepathic contact. They were perfect in every way, but not in any way I recognized. One of those beings ("angels" would be an inadequate description) welcomed me, and explained that I was being permitted to make a journey through the Kingdom of Heaven where no soul, still living in a material body, had been before. I was deeply affected by this, and said that I was ready to travel on.

I looked around. Everything was strange, and I instinctively knew that it was beautiful, but not in any earthly form. There were no paradise images: no flowers, no butterflies or animals, no palaces with fountains, and no palm beaches and blue sea. In short, every image that humans think of as being beautiful, peaceful, calm, and heavenly was not here. The whole scene made a deep impression on me, and the more I looked, the more I had the feeling I was looking at a gigantic landscape, divided into many sections. We went to an imaginary mountaintop, from which we viewed the surroundings. Beneath me there was a valley stretching as far as the eye could see. In the valley there were strange points, similar to the energy points I had seen before. They looked like small vibrating and pulsating spheres, and they made a humming noise. The valley was divided into two halves: one half was filled with white spheres, and the other half with black spheres.

The being leading the expedition said, "This is the Land of the Souls. What you see here are pure, complete souls, which are in the absolute reality of the Kingdom of Heaven, and therefore not in the Neutral Zone. These souls follow none of the evolutionary paths, and have none of the kind of lessons to learn you know about. They have other occupations and they 'are.'
As you can see, one half is white and the other black. This is to indicate what really happens here, and has nothing to do with positive or negative, or good and evil, as some people could presume. All the souls here are complete and divine, and have everything within them. There are neither karmas nor memories here. The black souls are identical to the white souls, but diametrically opposite. They belong to the anti-forces.

"The absolute reality of the Kingdom of Heaven consists of two systems, which complement each other and are opposites. The absolute true God controls them both, and is above these systems.

The two inverse systems create a perfect balance and interact with each other in order to propel evolution toward God. Without this, limited, interaction between the one, which is known to you, and the other inverse system, evolution could not take place."

I was silent because I understood that the truth was very complicated and the being continued, "We will now show you why and how a soul actually enters the Neutral Zone."

We "floated" toward the valley and, just above the borderline between the one system and the inverse system, we stopped. I saw individual souls on both sides.

"Watch carefully," the being said. "You will see something special." I saw that the souls closest to the borderline between the two systems seemed to be inquisitive. They seemed to be moving toward the souls on the opposite side. Each soul seemed both drawn to the opposite field, and yet aware that the opposite field was not for it. As soon as the soul had decided to investigate what was on the other side, a simple form of extra awareness developed to spur it on and move it away from its familiar and acceptable norms. This accelerated the journey toward the opposite field until it crossed the border. This meant that the soul was no longer among its fellow souls, but was alone in new surroundings. This was an enormous revelation to the soul, and led to a new awareness. Because it was unique in these new surroundings, the soul was able to view and assess itself. It had become aware.

At precisely that moment a control function came into force, and the souls, now permanently positioned in their opposite field, were taken away to a receiving station, whose function was to deal with the other souls which had crossed over, as it were.

The being said, "What you have seen is the mechanism that enables the souls to undertake a journey of awareness. This awareness is in all souls, on your Earth too. In the Christian religion this acquiring of knowledge and awareness is referred to as the 'Fall from Grace,' or 'Original Sin.' This is not an accurate term, because in reality this is a process, not of failure and disobedience, but rather of increased awareness and growth, which every soul will experience. Moreover this process takes place in Heaven, not in any of the universes of the Neutral Zone, and certainly not on your own planet. Once this has happened to the soul, it has a choice. It can develop this awareness of love for the divine Power, which is the rule in the Kingdom of Heaven. If it does this, the soul can continue to the other divine habitats within the reality of Heaven. The other choice is fuelled by curiosity for the unknown, and leads to resistance toward the divine powers. As you can see, the majority of the souls make this choice. Once this has been made, they are taken from the valley, and placed in a form of receiving station. From here they will go to the Neutral Zone to start the process of evolution, which will take them through all the phases of life and the lessons which go with them, until they return to the divine Creator and his eternal love."

We went to the receiving station, and I saw that this station was divided with one part in Heaven, and the other part in the Neutral Zone. The station was full of souls from both systems, placed here after their time of choice in the Land of Souls. They were sorted into groups. There the processes of evolution and their immediate future were explained to them. The souls did not listen to this, but were very impatient and could not wait to go into the Neutral Zone. I looked at this somewhat perplexed.

My companion explained, "There are many options in the Neutral Zone, and it is possible to follow all sorts of lessons and experiences. Once a certain choice in evolution has been made, it is not possible to change. The souls will continue on this path until the end of the evolution and the Neutral Zone can be left behind. On a future journey you will see this sorting process, and it will be possible to study the variety of the evolutionary possibilities, some of which are very strange. The journey you are allowed to undertake at present is designed to show you the absolute reality of the true Kingdom of Heaven."

We continued and, after a few moments, had left the receiving station and the Valley of the Souls far behind us. We floated high above a strange landscape, which was not a landscape as we would understand it, but an image of energy forms giving the impression of one. After a long journey we arrived in a strange place surrounded by high mountains. Purple-blue colors blended with a sky of deep dark red, glowing with orange and yellow suns. Beneath I saw strange creatures, which I could not identify from anything I knew. The whole was very grand.

We went down and stopped to look at these beings.

My companion spoke, "This part of the Kingdom of Heaven is the Land of the Dragons. The word 'dragons' is not correct of course, but I use this name because throughout the ages these creatures have been seen by men and appeared as the mythological dragons man talks of. Hence it is an easy term of reference. The dragons have tremendous energies and assist with very specific tasks, mainly to do with the protection of the souls incarnated on the planets. Dragons can assist in the great nuclear forces of the universe. As you can see they are strange creatures. They are really enormous concentrated masses of energy. On your planet you would call them plasma spheres in modern terms."

I watched the creatures deeply impressed. Some of these creatures approached us and by means of some form of brain contact it was possible to communicate. I had the feeling that I knew some of these creatures. I sensed trust, safety, and happiness there.

When it was time to leave, we floated again above the landscape, to a strange space, which appeared to be hollow, in as much as there was no form of any landscape. It was empty apart from many little lights. It resembled a starry sky against a deep dark blue, and yet light-emitting, background. In this space many strange beings appeared to be floating. They reminded me of seahorses and were roughly 2.5 meters long.

My companion said, "This is the Land of the Chormons and, as you can appreciate, this name too is not quite accurate. It was given to these creatures by someone from your planet, who saw them for the first time many centuries ago, and compared them with a mythological sea creature with a similar name. These beings are unique, because they have a very special and strange background. What you have seen is the complete, undivided soul (both the male and the female parts) present in the Valley of the Souls experiencing a variety of situations. Once they enter the Neutral Zone, the souls are divided at a certain point in their evolution. You will learn this on a different journey. The complete undivided soul, which is in the Valley of the Souls, can also join its opposite number in the anti-system. If both agree to this, a being is created, which consists of two complete souls complementary to each other or four half souls joined together. The result is the being that you now see before you. They are above the system of the two opposite fields, and are apart from any evolution within the Neutral Zone. They have no mode of reaction and are therefore extremely suited for very specific tasks and duties within the system. It is possible for them to incarnate into a human body, and they do so frequently. These people are then spiritual teachers or have other tasks, which you are unable to comprehend. Because of their inert nature they can avoid the normal problems and pitfalls, which are part of everyday life, but they come and go from their chosen incarnation." We stayed a while with these beings, and I learned more about their strange history.

We bade our farewells, left the chormons, and continued the journey. After a while we arrived at a strange landscape. It was very quiet, and nothing moved.

My companion said, "This is the Land without Souls and where only the Gods are allowed to enter. You cannot go in there. The only reason we have shown you it is to let you know that it exists."

I watched a long time. The strange colors and scenes both caused nausea and had a hypnotic effect. Yet I had a great desire to go in and investigate this, because I felt that many secrets were hidden in there.

"Do not try to go in there," my companion warned, "because it is not permitted. You will learn about it in the future."

We continued our journey, and floated high above endless habitats where things were happening, which I cannot describe, because they have no description known in our world. The closest would be to describe them as nuclear processes. After a while we stopped at a large gate, which was closed, but as soon as we stopped, it opened quietly. We went through the gate, but after a few steps had to stop.

My companion said, "It is permitted that you take a look inside, but you are not allowed to go further. This is the Land of the Gods."

I looked at him questioningly and he continued, "The meaning and expression of God is something that is not understood by men. God is imagined as a being in your religions and philosophies. This is not the case. The real and absolute God is something that can be understood neither by you, nor by anyone else. Between the absolute God and the souls, there are other beings called gods, but this word has nothing to do with the real God. These beings are responsible for the workings of all the planets and the star systems in any of the universes. They are often perceived by humans as God, and indeed humanity has often communicated with them. This is their habitat. They are larger than normal souls, but smaller than God, and are also responsible to the absolute God."

I looked for a long time at this place, and its beauty was overpowering. It appeared somewhat like a landscape in soft pastel colors, with shapes like clouds and mist.

After a while we moved on, while my companion explained, "You have been allowed to see a small part of the true Kingdom of Heaven. You understand a great deal, but you must realize that your material brain cannot process most of what you have seen. You are allowed to keep the memory of all you have seen, but it will be difficult to describe it. Do you have any questions?"

"Yes," I answered, and my companion smiled as he had already guessed my question. "You are searching for the highest, and you understand that this is difficult. It is permitted to every soul who seeks, and is found ready, but you will not be allowed to keep any memory of the details – only the memory and the impression that you actually made this step. Is this clear to you?"

I nodded in agreement because I knew the spiritual law that no soul still living in a mortal body could retain the detail of Heaven.

"Go and may the love of God enlighten your steps. It is the only condition here that counts. Nothing else is tolerated. Do not doubt, be strong, and do not let any thoughts of darkness enter your thinking."

My companion left, and I had to continue along on a path, which was a form of bridge. Both sides of the path appeared as a deep abyss full of light. Everywhere around me was light, and in front of me, my goal, so bright that it dazzled me, and I could not see through it. I continued and reached the goal, which I had determined to find. After a while I returned silently to the group of beings who had accompanied me, and who were waiting patiently. They did not ask, nor did they speak, but we understood. Quietly we continued our journey through the absolute reality and after a while we approached the borders of the Neutral Zone. I said goodbye to my companions. This goodbye was emotional, but we knew that we would meet again in the future.

The beings sent me over the border, where the angel had been waiting patiently. Once across, I felt sad and lonely, and was quiet. Noticing this, the angel enquired as to why I felt so sad. I told her that I felt a sense of loss. She smiled and said, "Come. I will show you something."

She put her hands on my eyes, and I could feel a change by the warmth of her hands. This time I saw a vision of the future, which made me happy.

She continued, "As you can see you have a lot to do. You will experience much, but you will also find great happiness. Take your role and your task and do this well. You will get a lot of help, more then you think possible, and now you know what is in store for you."

I was quiet and, after a long trip, we arrived at the little planet, Earth. The angel said goodbye with the words, "This goodbye is not for long because I will come and get you 'tomorrow' for a new journey. Then we will study the evolutionary opportunities in the Neutral Zone."

v i s i o n

The soul journey

On this journey I was led by the angel who had accompanied me through the Neutral Zone, to the borders of the Kingdom of Heaven.

She took me by the hand saying, "We will now travel through the Neutral Zone and I will show you the path which has to be completed by the soul from the moment it arrives here until it leaves. In other words, you will see the whole of evolution. This is not all; you will see other evolutionary possibilities as well. The soul has a choice about how its evolution will proceed, but once this choice has been made, it cannot be altered. The complete journey has to be followed. This choice is one of the factors which influence life, and how a body or soul will be."

We went through infinite space, and after a long journey, we arrived at the receiving station of the souls. It was the same station that I had seen on a previous journey but on that occasion I was looking at it from the outside. This time I was approaching it from a different direction, from inside the Neutral Zone.

The angel spoke. "Watch carefully because what happens now is very important. As you know the souls arrive here once they have completed the journey in the inverse field. This process separates them from the Kingdom of Heaven, and it is essential that they experience a number of different forms of awareness while they are in the Neutral Zone."

We went further into the receiving station and noticed that there were many completed (i.e. undivided) souls, from both the main system and the inverse system. It was interesting to notice that there was no longer any difference between them. They were all the same, which is possibly why this place was called the Neutral Zone. The souls were now divided into groups, which remained together during this period of choosing their evolutionary path. There were many possible paths. The system to which I belonged, and along with me the whole of planet Earth and the immediate system we can see in the visible cosmos, was an evolutionary process of seven stages. By means of seven separate lessons, possibilities, or circumstances, souls are made aware of the truth. In between each of the stages of this evolution there was a short interval called Changes or Passing. I was aware also of other evolutionary possibilities, which were completely different from the one we experience ourselves. There were other paths with three stages, nine stages, twelve stages, twenty-four stages, thirty-nine stages, and also one without any stage at all, but which was continuous.

The angel said, "These evolutionary processes are separate from each other and have, in principle, nothing to do with each other at any point. The separation takes place by means of a procedure, which is one of the nine dimensions. We will now follow the evolutionary process which you are part of. This is the path with seven stages, and we will go to the beginning of the first stage. You have already experienced this in your thinking, as a few million years ago. As you can see, evolution is continuous. In other words, new souls are continuously entering this process, and you will now be able to see what this means."

We entered a strange space, which I was unable to define. It was not a space in the usual meaning of the word, but it appeared as a strange mixture of energies and colors. These energies were moving and crystallized into forms that I could not describe. I saw the souls, which had yet to experience their first lessons, enter the space, and I could hear cries of happiness.

"Freedom!" they exclaimed. Here the souls had various experiences, which bore no relation to anything I had ever encountered. The energy forms were used to build the most wondrous scenes and systems. Souls lived like little children in a play park for the first time. It was not negative, low, or bad. It was extremely good fun to watch. Everyone was playing to their heart's content. I stood and watched this rather amused, but the angel explained that there was a serious purpose behind the levity.

"This is a stage during which the souls will experience their first freedom. This stage is designed to take off the sharp edges of human life. Extreme experiences occur here but they do not do any real damage. Nothing really happens in this stage, but if this part did not exist, the next stage would be much more complicated. The soul must learn to handle this freedom without doing any damage."

I understood this and we progressed toward the end of this stage.

The angel said, "What you will learn now is of great importance. You will experience the change from the first stage to the second, and during it something important takes place. Watch carefully."

I did so, and I saw that virtually all the souls from the first stage had now gathered in some form of space. Strange beings arrived, beings that I had encountered on previous travels, but whom I could not as yet identify. They were always silent. There was no communication of any kind as they worked. They took the souls and divided them into two parts. Each part had its own attributes, but they needed each other to be whole again. Next they received a spiritual body, which was a dense form of the soul. The spirits or souls, which had now been divided, stood and watched amazed at themselves, and at each other. There were marked differences, but the most important was the fact that the spirit body was built in such a way that one could distinguish the future of each person. They were granted additional awareness and knowledge, and then the souls or spirits were allowed to enter the second stage or period.

The angel said, "This event is essential. The aim of the soul is to learn divine love in all its glory and understand the twists and turns that life brings. The complete, undivided soul, as you saw in the first period, will never learn this on its own and is incapable of achieving this because it is driven by its innate resistance mechanism, which brought it here in the first place. Think back to your previous journeys when you saw the souls in their opposite fields. A soul could continue in its separated way until it no longer had any knowledge of where it came from. The Creator does not allow this to happen, and the dividing of the souls into two halves is an essential process, which enables the soul to learn that one half needs the other. Each soul half is imbalanced in energy terms and will search for its counterpart to re-unite. As you can see, it is not made easy to recognize each other, and a certain amount of effort is required. The souls also experience the normal feelings of men and women even if in primitive form. Watch carefully."

I looked again and saw that the now divided souls in their spiritual bodies, yet resembling men and women, entered a strange landscape. It would be considered a spiritual area, for images appeared that were not material. The place was vast and not constrained by the limitations of a planet. The souls now had the opportunity to live out their feelings and desires. Soon a wild chase developed to find the missing half, but this was difficult since the counterpart was not easy to recognize. The souls also discovered that their other halves, once found, differed in beauty and attractiveness. A strange game developed during which a variety of feelings, including desire and lust, emerged. The missing half, as well as the availability of other halves of varying beauty, triggered primitive forms of love, desire, jealousy, and hatred. Fights broke out because the souls envied the property of others and desired other soul halves. This resulted in very strange scenes. Violent fights and murder blew up, but since the souls had only a spirit and no material body, there was no serious outcome. With a murder there was no victim, and with rape or torture there was no pain. Love was expressed in strange ways: the entire scene was bizarre.

Other events were also going on. Souls were trying to build a variety of technologies, but did not succeed because there was no matter with which to accomplish this.

The angel spoke again saying, "As you can see, the second period is very difficult without creating any real damage. The changes to the souls have given them a number of goals and purposes, but since they do not understand love, and especially divine love, scenes like the ones you see now are commonplace. They do not have a material body, and therefore cannot do any damage, and so experience neither guilt nor karma. From a divine point of view the crimes committed are real, but in spirit form the souls can use these situations to work on their spiritual development without any real fear or damage. In this period they can take the first steps on a path that will bring them in the end to purification. The next period of sorrow would be much more intense if their deeds had been 'real.'"

We moved slowly toward the end of this stage, and noticed that, yet again, a change occurred, which transported the souls from the second to the third stage. During this change another operation took place. This time it became necessary that souls lived in a specific habitat, and that they had to use a material body in order to live, work, and learn. They worked small pieces of land in order to learn.

I saw that a universe was created in which there was a wide variety of stars and planets, which housed these pieces of land. The planets were suitable for the human bodies, animals, and plant life. The souls had to enter these bodies as some form of spacesuit, and had to use this body to learn and experience what they had already encountered during the first two stages. There was a small group of planets (twelve to be exact), first inhabited by human bodies, which were made alive by the souls entering them as spirits. All other souls had to wait for a while. The strangeness of this process was increased by a mist surrounding it.

The angel spoke, "The gods, whose habitat you were allowed to see during your earlier journey, are responsible for the placing of the correct bodies on the appropriate planets. However, it is not permitted for you to see this process."

I could understand this perfectly, since real knowledge of the creation of bodies would be abused by mankind.

I saw that the incarnated souls reproduced rapidly, and by using the knowledge and awareness given to them by their Creator, they were able to develop very fast and create an amazing technology. This enabled them to move across the entire universe, populating the suitable planets. Spiritual and divine love were ignored, and it was clear that the same scenes I had observed in the first two stages would be repeated, but with devastating and bloody consequences. Not only on a personal level, but also on a universal scale, the hatred and envy was so great that it led to full-scale wars between various planets. They only stopped when every resource had been exhausted, and there was nothing left to fight with. The planets were empty and desolate. Only a few human creatures remained, and once again each planet, with its own inhabitants, had to develop from nothing.

The angel went on to explain, "All you have seen has also been experienced by yourself. Life in the third stage is the most intensive. This is because everything is now experienced as real. The spiritual awareness of men is not yet developed and only near the end of this, the third period, will men be aware of God and their own divine spirit. That is the lesson of the third period, which is now almost over for you. On the next journey you will see the history of the third period in detail, which, after all, is your own history. We will now venture toward the end of the third period, which will interest you because it is your own future you will experience."

We went to the end of this period, and I saw a section of the visible universe and in it, many star systems, stars, and planets. It was vibrating and pulsating to a particular harmony. Suddenly there was a sea of light, and strange beings operating on a different frequency shifted the whole into a new state of harmony. I saw twelve star systems, one of which was the Milky Way, changing in strong energy bursts. Everything was now vibrating a little faster. Practically speaking, this meant that many material entities were removed and altered. Similar changes took place on planets like Earth, and these were experienced by its inhabitants as disasters. However, from a divine point of view they were not real disasters.

The old system was severely shaken up and renewed and a lot of detritus was thrown out. A tidy, cleaned up, and fully renewed system was now suitable for the lessons of the soul in the new, fourth period of evolution. All souls, which had left their material body at the end of the third period, were collected in some form of receiving station. Here they were taught about the events that had taken place in the third period. Everything was reviewed, conclusions were drawn, and much became clear to them. The souls received new goals and instructions, the main one of which was developing, experiencing, and applying divine love toward the Creator and fellow human beings. Many freedoms had to be curbed, especially in relationships. Special attention was paid to the fact that unification with the missing spiritual half was now imminent, and this was the lesson of the fourth period.

The angel said, "This is now your future, but for other souls this is already past, because the process is continuous. As you can see, the fourth period is in a material sense virtually identical to the third period, but the freedom of the third period is no longer an option. Men have to learn and the Creator will not let them continue to behave irresponsibly."

I looked again at the history of the fourth period, which now lay ahead of us. I could only see the broad spectrum and discovered that here also many problems lay ahead. Mankind often looks toward the new era as a heavenly paradise where everything is "perfect," and the mistakes of the past are no longer made. Unfortunately this is not the case. The fourth period is only one of the stages in the true evolution toward the light, and has its own share of problems. The beginning of the end of this period already began during the early years, and while this period is really more beautiful and loving than the third, it is not perfect.

We floated toward the move between the fourth stage and the fifth, and I discovered that the material bodies had now transformed in a manner such that I could no longer recognize them as material bodies. The many dimensions, which influence each creation, were already so altered from the known systems that they were no longer recognizable. What I noticed was that there was a form of escape mechanism built into the process, which a soul was able to use at any moment and at any point, in any stage during its journey. If the soul was spiritually aware of its divine origins, and had understood divine love in all its forms, it was then possible to leave the entire evolutionary path and return to Heaven where the angels were waiting. In other words, the duration and intensity of the journey was determined by the souls and not by God. It is not possible ever to blame God for what happens. A soul could stay on the path by exercising free will, or leave by being aware of the mechanism to leave. This actually happened, and it was clear that at the end of the fourth period, and certainly after the fifth, many souls had left the system. Fewer and fewer were still learning. They had learned their spiritual lessons and were united in the light. Only the most severe cases had to go on until the change to the sixth period. This change was almost silent, but there was an important difference. The souls had now only a spirit body and no longer a material body. This situation was similar to that of the second stage of the evolution. This brought enlightenment but also restrictions. The lessons, which had been easy during the fourth and fifth period, were now very difficult. In other words, the longer one took to become aware, the more difficult it was to complete the journey. Despite the difficulties many souls succeeded in learning the lessons and at the point that the sixth stage had finished and the seventh began, there were only a few left with any lessons to learn at all.

In the seventh period also, the spirit body had to be surrendered, and the lessons could now only be learned as pure but divided souls. This brought many difficulties, as the learning here took the form of pure energy, and no visible scene could be distinguished.

The seventh period was the only one with no pre-determined length. This stage was completed once the last souls had made the final step toward divine love.

The angel spoke once more, "At this point evolution is completed and all souls in this group are brought back to the divine Light. What will happen then will be impossible for you to understand at the moment, but will be made clear in your future. But, as you can see, evolution is continuous, since there are new souls brought here by the separation at the Neutral Zone.

"You may see that all of the creations are static and motionless, and that only the souls move through the creation like moving through the scenes of a film. You may imagine that for instance, on a different level, the Second World War is still ongoing but with different souls. The motion of the soul through evolution is then the driving force, which is experienced as time. This is complicated, but you will be allowed to experience this in a separate journey, during which you will see every dimension. Then it will all be clear."

We continued our journey, and I could see the whole universe again. We stopped and watched the whole creation for a long time. It was only one of the many creations and expressions of the Creator. We discussed various subjects and the angel said, "You have now seen the evolutionary paths that are possible for the soul, and you have seen your own evolution in great detail. It is not essential for you to see every variation of opportunity. They would be incomprehensible to you, but it is of importance that you know that they exist. We will now return to Earth, and next time you will undertake a new journey."

After this long and interesting journey through the past, the present, and the future, which I learned were in fact all continuous, I returned in my body to Earth.

vision

The human journey

I was taken to a movie theatre by a being of light. There were no other people present and I sat very comfortably.

The angel spoke, "It is important that you have a better understanding of many situations in life and we will therefore show you a section of the past, and another of the future. This is not a simple history lesson, but a spiritual message of divine love. You will see this in the form of a 'newsreel.' Watch carefully and you will be given a special lesson."

The light went out and the "film" started. What appeared in front of me was the planet Earth, and I saw how life was created. It moved very quickly, as if in fast forward mode. I saw the development of Earth as a sort of "terraforming." From a barren, volcanic planet were created the first life forms, whose purpose was to reduce the poison in the atmosphere. It was like a chain reaction: the first primitive life forms began to develop, the planet cooled quickly, and the oceans were filled with small creatures, which grew into very large animals. I saw Earth become green and fill with trees, shrubs, grasses, and flowers. The atmosphere changed, and a blue sky with a very bright, almost white, Sun created a very special picture. It affected me deeply, and I thought how beautiful this was, untouched by humans. From the oceans and the plants came the first life forms, resembling animals, although I did not recognize them. They certainly did not look like the dinosaurs I had seen in books. More importantly, during the entire film of the development of the earth not a single dinosaur,

115

in the known sense of the word, appeared. There were many large creatures, which looked entirely different from each other, but they were not familiar to me. An entire evolution took place in the vision in front of me: some creatures disappeared while others made their first appearance.

At a specific moment I became aware of a large fertile plain, bordered on one side by a sea, and on the other side by mountains. It was a beautiful plain with lots of grass, trees, and flowers and a bare section of sand. On the horizon silver dots appeared, which came closer and closer very quickly. Once they were very near, I saw that they were "planes," and they landed on the landform, which I had just seen. There were twenty-five of these planes, and out of them came strange beings. They looked like normal humans, and gradually they began to populate the world. Other beings of different appearance came, and steadily all these groups spread across the world. Whilst most of these beings resembled humans, they differed from each other. It was interesting to note that they brought with them their own cultures. Some of the beings did not look at all like humans, but lived in seas, or disappeared into the mountains.

The development of the planet continued but, from time to time, was interrupted by great natural disasters, which were a devastation for those who lived in the area where they occurred. A massive comet struck the Earth and wiped out virtually all forms of life. On another occasion the magnetic poles moved and the resulting changes caused massive earthquakes, as well as many other types of disaster. All these events shaped the planet in different ways, and its appearance changed beyond recognition. There was now little dry land left. As a result of the impact of some large comets, the water levels had risen sharply.

The humans showed a remarkable resistance, and after each event rebuilt their environment. New people inhabited the Earth in ever-changing appearances and numbers. Mankind had all sorts of problems to endure, and from these difficulties they learned. Until this point there had only been natural and cosmic disasters altering the face of the planet, but that too changed. Mankind left its own marks through, for instance, the use of fire. People increased their knowledge, became clever, and built a vast technological society. They also envied the land and possessions of others, and embarked on wars fuelled by jealousy. The wars in turn caused changes in many parts of the world. Eventually a war broke out akin to a nuclear war. Massive explosions were detonated, and humanity was almost completely destroyed. The Earth was now barren and empty again, and all the beauty that I had seen at the beginning of the film, had disappeared.

A few humans had survived and they tried in a desperate way to stay alive by eating insects and animals, because plants no longer grew. Evolution started again, but this time more quickly, and from this long-gone era new civilizations were born. Large areas of land were inhabited once again by people with knowledge of technology. But each time a civilization reached the peak of its development a kind of resentment, unhappiness, and superiority grew in the people, and they brought about their own destruction. I saw that many civilizations had disappeared in this way. The names Atlantis and Lemuria came into my head. I learned also the names of many civilizations, which I had never heard of before, and which I did not know from legends and myths. These civilizations must have been destroyed so completely that there were no traces left, not even in the stories. I saw floods cover the planet periodically. Life was not easy for humanity. I also saw that help came time after time from other planets. These populations provided assistance to rebuild the lives and societies on Earth. Once this was done, they would disappear again. The "film" then showed scenes that were more recognizable. I saw civilizations like those in Greece, Egypt, China, and India. From here new people emerged, and slowly, scene by scene, we arrived at history which is reasonably well known. I saw the Roman Empire, Christ, the Middle Ages, and also the First and the Second World Wars. I understood the real meaning of these events in a spiritual sense, when finally this part of the "film" was over.

There was a break, and the lights went on as my companion said, "What you have seen is an outline of the history of the planet on which you live. It is the history of the third evolutionary period and, as you know, there are still four to come. You have already completed two. On other planets in the universe similar evolutions have taken place but, of course, in a different fashion, and with different lessons. It is God's purpose that each possible situation is created in the universe in order to provide opportunities for the soul to learn and experience. Through this the soul enriches its existence and grows. The love of the Creator has no end. It is all patience. If you cannot find a certain lesson, it will be created for you. Also, if you have any desire for a particular challenge, then time and opportunity are provided in order to help you reach understanding. The divine purposes, however, are not always the wishes and desires of mankind, and that is why problems emerge. This period has been given to you, with all its freedom, to create and experience all you want – you even have the freedom to resist the divine love. Yet lessons will have to be learned, and every soul must experience this. This is the reason why you saw that every time man thinks he has reached his peak, and thinks he does not need spiritual help, something happens that will thwart his plan. Men may think and hope that they can do it all by themselves, but they are assisted in their efforts by the divine hand of God.

"At the moment when man thinks that his goal is reached the divine hand is sometimes removed and disaster strikes. This only happens because mankind has become superior and arrogant. If divine help has been recognized, thankfully received, and experienced, no problems will occur, and human society can continue. This is an important first lesson."

I smiled, remembering the legend of Odysseus, who thought that he was strong, and could do without the gods, only to realize what he had to learn on a long, difficult journey before he could enjoy love again. It was a hard and dangerous journey abounding in lessons. Suddenly I understood these old legends. The journey of Odysseus, no less then the journey of men throughout life, teaches the lesson not to abandon the gods or divine love. Faith and trust are vital.

The angel continued, "The first and most important lesson in the third period of the evolution of the soul is the recognition of the divine hand and its protection in all of existence. Everything will be given to the soul if it cooperates with the Creator, but will be removed if taken for granted and rejected. Do you understand this?"

I did. This lesson was very clear indeed.

The being continued, "There are many other lessons to learn, and, as soon as the soul acknowledges the hand of God, spiritual awareness will be revealed as well as divine love. Experiencing these lessons, however, is not possible in the present environment, and this must therefore be changed. This is the move to the fourth period of the evolution of the soul and will happen quickly. You know that many people have a leaning toward this, but they do not fully understand. They think, expect, and in some cases even hope, that the Earth will be struck by war, pestilence, and problems, and that on the foundations of the remnants of such a disaster a 'New Jerusalem' will be built. This way of thinking is wrong because the truth is different. Divine love is absolute love and no sorrow or problems exist within it.

"God means no harm, but souls make their own futures. They will reap that what they have sown over many ages, and through God's love each soul will get the chance to experience this love and to grow. This divine love provides a new opportunity but it will mean, practically speaking, that there will be many problems of man's making, since every lesson has to be gone through. There are no shortcuts. Therefore there will be wars and natural disasters for those who have created them. However, be aware that it is not good to live in fear of those situations that are not meant for you. Everything that will happen to you is already locked inside you, and you will garner what you have sown. It is not good to prophesize because it is not doom that awaits. Only deliverance is the future, but its form may not be what one expects. You may fear something you do not understand. This can bring about a change, but it is not a disaster, even though many people in the material world will experience it as such.

"Fear of losing something is your greatest enemy. It might be fear of losing money, property, house, job, even life. The life-changing event is not the problem, since this acts as the purification for the soul."

I was silent and indicated that I understood everything.

The being continued, "You will now see the second part of the film, the future. It is strange since it is not understood by anyone

119

on Earth, because their way of thinking is too limited. Watch carefully."

The lights went out, and the images began again. I saw events including some I had experienced myself. It was strange because I saw that fear in the world held people in its grip. Strangely these fears were not real but were created by mankind itself. I saw fear of wars and nuclear weapons, and also fear about job security, and fear of death. In short, all the fears known to men, but none of it was real. Many of the fears were even created and maintained with a great deal of effort since people unconsciously found it was impossible to live without them. People clamped themselves to these fears. Fear was part of their existence, and was clearly exploited by others. Many problems, such as the east-west relationships in the world, were not real but were kept prominent, because they were important for a small group of people who benefited. Mankind was fooling itself by creating unnecessary fear. I saw a battery of nuclear rockets, which were used by one half of the earth to threaten the other half, but the rockets were empty and did not function. I saw the bizarre stage play of the twentieth century, and I realized that God had said, "Now it is enough. This cluttering cannot continue since one lie is only there because of another lie. Lies become a form of truth. The right path is missing and I will bring light again."

I saw that the entire universe was now subjected to a change, and all matter along with spiritual manifestations was vibrating a little faster. Each star and each planet was altered and cleaned up, and lies could no longer thrive. Everything was now vibrating and pulsating differently, and one could see through the deceit to find real truth. It was a tremendous shock to realize this, since matter had obscured the truth. Each individual soul was now graded and, depending on the outcome, lessons had to be learned. The universe rocked, and where the lies were greatest, the largest changes took place in the form of material disasters. Where fear was greatest, the disaster was largest. Everything sown in lack of awareness was now harvested, and mankind screamed for help. They blamed God. They said that they had not known, and that they had acted in good faith.

But the Creator replied, "The path to divine love has always been there. Many lessons over many eras have been given to you, but you did not listen and did not try to understand. Although it is not possible in this period to see the spiritual nature of things, that does not mean that it does not exist. Do not think for a moment that you are alone, since I see you every day and every hour and every second. I know your entire soul, and you cannot hide anything from me. Do not kid yourself, others and most importantly, me, and do not think that no one can see into your behavior. The lesson in this period was the recognition and acceptance of the divine love under blind circumstances. It is easy to believe in this, and to trust if one is experiencing it on a daily basis, but it is very difficult if one sees nothing. You can hear if you have ears and see if you have eyes. Only those who can do this have experienced me, and found divine love, but because you cannot see this in the material world, do not think that it is not there."

After a while the whole scene came to rest, but everything was different now, and the stars, planets, and star systems had a brighter and cleaner appearance. Many individuals had to surrender their earthly body, not only on Earth, but also on other inhabited planets as this event had caused numerous physical deaths. The event was cosmic and certainly not limited to Earth. Even in the matter of disasters mankind had been arrogant, as in reality Earth was only one of the many planets that experienced this change. The souls, which had left their material bodies, were sent to a kind of school to be educated. Few people were left, and it reminded me of situations that I had seen in the first part of the film. I began to think that the event was a form of cycle.

I knew that I would get answers to all my questions and so I was silent, and turned again toward the screen to watch the film. I saw a planet, which was radiant and bright, and knew that this was the Earth but not the old Earth. It was a planet with the incarnation of the soul of the old planet (present-day Earth), which had now died. It was very beautiful in rich, bright colors. No human hand had touched this planet. It had been given to us all as a new, clean system to learn our next lessons. I saw that the beings that had survived the changeover in their physical forms, now lived on this planet to learn. After a while they spread, and the population expanded, as all the souls that had lived before were now reincarnated in those new

bodies. The lessons, which were part of the new and fourth period, were simple enough for those who understood, but proved difficult for mankind. They were the development of:
- the divine Love for the Creator, the complementary soul half, and fellow beings;
- the development of the original divine gifts from this divine love;
- the development, from the divine love, of working with the environment and harmonizing with nature; and
- the unification with the soul complement.

I saw that life developed, and that humanity learned and experienced the many lessons that were in store for it. In this stage some mistakes were made. The Creator did not mind since His patience was great. He ensured that every soul received all the opportunities it needed, and that He would keep the system for as long as it would take, until every soul enjoyed the love of God. I saw some of the history of this new period, but only in broad outline. It was obviously not good for me to know the future in great detail. The film was now finished, and the lights went on again.

The being, which had kept me company during all this time, spoke, "You have now seen the present, the past, and a glimpse of the future. This is given to you so you can understand what is happening. You will be given many more lessons, and you will be allowed to make many and strange journeys. The purpose of this is so that you can provide guidance to others. Remember, however, that the future is something determined by the soul. From a spiritual point of view there will be many changes, as you have seen, but how this fits into the material world is determined by each being. It is therefore not good to see the future as a doom-laden scenario. Ponder deeply as what I will be saying now is important. It is impossible for a human to see into the future because God will not allow this to happen. The future is locked in each soul and is the result of one's actions. One may have a precognition or feeling about the future, but this is not a prophecy. Only the soul itself knows what it will have to experience. What the soul has sown, the soul will harvest. Nothing can change this. Everyone always makes his or her own future. How this will turn out in the material world for each person is neither your problem, nor your responsibility.

"As I have said, each individual is responsible for his or her own actions. The future will be strange and difficult, but think about what I have said, since this is also a promise, and God will allow no harm. If you have nothing to fear, then nothing frightening will happen. This is quite different from that which mankind may think."

I had understood the lesson. Furthermore, I could understand that the real problems for the human race were different from what they currently thought. Mankind had got stuck in the material world, and experienced this as his only reality. That is why there will continue to be events, which are not pleasant, but from an absolute point of view are not disasters.

vision

Time mechanisms and anti-forces

I was taken to the Sun by an angel who had been my companion on previous journeys. Before we set out, she said, "You are going to witness an interesting event. It will be interesting for you, because it is about a truth you do not yet know, and will find very strange. For us it is an everyday event.

"As you know, a variety of evolutions take place on the planet you call Earth, and on all the other planets in this solar system, and the Sun itself. These evolutionary processes are not always concerned with life as you imagine it but, in the main, deal with other processes of change, which you do not yet understand. Similar processes take place on planets that are part of other stars in the universe. These processes are neither continuous, nor independent. If they were, then within a short time everything would be out of control. But the system needs attention. Just like a well-oiled machine, it must be adjusted once in a while. You may see this as an interactive control system, which, on your planet, can be viewed as a feedback mechanism. In other words, the divine powers interfere depending on the developments that take place. Watch carefully, because you will see something few have witnessed."

More angels came, accompanied by beings I had seen earlier in the Kingdom of Heaven. They went to the Sun, and stopped it. Immediately the planets and their satellites stopped as well, and nothing moved. We went toward Earth, and I saw that all was frozen in time. There too nothing moved. All was still. Even a bird was stopped in flight. It was bizarre to be able to walk through a city, or a landscape, without being noticed by the many people there, who just stood still. The angels and the heavenly beings started their work. They carried out a variety of tasks, best described as energy balancing of the evolutionary programs and patterns. This took an enormous amount of time. The complete overhaul took a period, which, if it could be measured, would be approximately 500 years. During this period, however, everything was stopped, and did not change, or age, in any way.

When the work was finished, the angel and the heavenly beings traveled toward the Sun, and started the process once more. Much to my amazement, everything on Earth came alive again. All the beings, which had been frozen, continued as if nothing had happened. It was simply not noticed that there had been a time vacuum, or subroutine, of almost 500 years. No time had passed for the living creatures in the material world, and they continued their life happily.

The angel explained: "What you have seen was essential, because you can see that sometimes situations must be adjusted. If normal life continued, then these adjustments could not take place, and a lot of damage could be inflicted on humanity. The divine driving force is therefore stopped for a while out of safety. This happens often and, depending on the periods and situations on Earth, it can take place several times a year. These events do not always take as long as this one, and sometimes not even longer than a few days but, in some cases, may take a thousand years."

I wondered if it was possible to experience such an event and be aware of it.

In response the angel said, "It is sometimes possible to take part in these events, but it is impossible to have a memory of them. Moreover, it creates problems. First of all you must be in the same position immediately before, and directly after, the event. If your body is not in the same position, then it will be torn apart by the forces which reposition it. Even if your arm was only about 1 centimeter out of its position, for example, then there would be a problem. The movement at the moment that the mechanism started again is faster than light, and the arm would be torn apart, or at the very least, suffer an enormous shock.

"Also the ageing process is significant. Once you take part in the process, you will age, because your time will run with our time, and not your own time, which has been stopped. Do you understand this?"

I did so, but had another question. It concerned an experience that I had had, when I seemed to go back in time approximately 900 years. This experience was physical. I could remember it very well, and it had left me with many questions.

The angel spoke, "The meaning of time is not easy but, under certain circumstances, it is possible that you have a connection with the future and the past. It is for you impossible to travel physically to the future, or the past, within your own evolution. That is only possible within the spirit. This is not only because of the so-called causality principles, which your scientists think they understand, but is also for another important reason.

"The soul is eternal, and is in a human body, within the spiritual habitats, or in the Kingdom of Heaven, and it is simply not possible to break through your spiritual evolution. If you were to break through this, and travel perhaps 1000 years forward or backward, you would need to duplicate your own soul, since it has already been there a thousand years ago, but in a different existence. Your scientists, who can think only in material worlds, do not consider this. Rather they create complicated mathematics to describe something that it is impossible to describe anyway. Only your eternal soul determines the freedom of your existence. Yet it is seemingly possible to travel through time without violating all these laws, and this you have experienced many times. Under certain circumstances it is possible that you are connected with the direct evolutionary waves, which are either behind or in front of you, but are not part of your own path. This is not true time traveling, as there is no forward or backward movement, but rather a sideways movement. It is how you can experience a situation, which is already past, or will become future, on your own evolutionary route. As you have seen in previous lessons, evolution is a continuous process with new souls constantly embarking on their journey. I mentioned as an example the Second World War, which is still raging, but with completely new souls, which have nothing to do with you. Thus everything in history is present and future at the same time, but with different souls experiencing it.

"It is possible that you decide to bring a spiritual or material lesson to a group of people, and it is possible to physically and materially travel on this other evolutionary path. You experience this as time travel, but it is not. The scenes you see look like past or future, but are in reality the present for the souls experiencing them. This is what you have encountered in your reality.

"In the history of mankind there are many examples of people who assisted, and teachers, who came without warning and then disappeared. Do you understand this process?"

I indicated that I had understood everything I had been told. In reality there was nothing really like past, present, or future, but only our own movement in a stage play. In the experience I enquired about, I had obviously connected with an evolution, which, compared to our own, was 900 years in the past, but yet was still the present.

The angel spoke again, "There is more to know yet. The soul is in reality very difficult for humanity to imagine. Past, present, and future are rather strange, and the fact that so many universes, worlds, and evolutionary waves are running through each other does not make it easy for you to understand everything thoroughly. It is not surprising that most of humanity does not know, and is not aware. For the moment you have seen and experienced enough, and it is important that you make the next journey."

The angel took me by the hand, and we floated through the Neutral Zone. A range of star systems was visible, a view now well known to me. At one point we stood on a mountaintop (again not a real mountain, but it appeared this way), and we could see over the entire Neutral Zone to all the universes. But this time the view was different: stronger and clearer. It was also possible to see the individual star systems within a universe, and also a part of the real Kingdom of Heaven. By some means it was also possible to see a connection between all I could see, but I had no words describe this.

The angel said, "On your previous journeys you have seen the anti-forces from a distance. Now you will enter the inverse field of the anti-forces for a short journey, but remember that this is something that is not possible under normal circumstances. Because you are searching and have questions, and you are the only one who can do this, it will be shown to you, but it is very difficult to understand. Are you ready?" I said yes but wondered secretly if one was ever ready for something one did not understand.

The angel noticed my reaction and smiled. "Have no fear because you will now experience an interesting situation," she said.

We floated further and, in front of me, I saw a strange shadow looming. It looked like a translucent cloud of purple; dark colors with some red and blue. Although it looked frightening, I did not feel any fear. The angel said, "The anti-forces are, from an energy point of view, opposite, but not negative, and certainly have nothing to do with evil. The reason you see this as black and negative is the fact that that is how you experience this inverse field while you are still in your own system."

We continued and the looming mass was now so big that it seemed to engulf everything. The Neutral Zone, with all its universes as I knew them, was no longer visible and in front of me I saw only a black mass. We came to the borderline and I felt strange at the moment I entered the inverse field. My faithful companion was no longer there. I was shocked and turned around looking for her. She was just before the borderline of the inverse field, but she could not continue, and stood waiting.

Then I heard a voice. I turned again to see a being, which, strangely enough, looked very familiar to me. This being, resembling but not identical to an angel, explained, "I will accompany you on your journey through the inverse field with the anti-forces. I am the complement of the angel who has accompanied you so far. She cannot enter the inverse field without causing problems. I will therefore now take you further because I am also familiar with your journey."

I was silent, filled with many questions, but the angel went on to say, "I can understand your questions, but have a little patience, and you will get answers to all of them. You will now make a journey through the inverse field. Watch carefully, because you will never see it again."

We moved forwards, and slowly an odd change spread over the surroundings. The dark colors, which looked frightening a while ago, were now different, as the entire scene in the inverse field became visible. It was a very strange revelation because everything I knew was also in this system, but in a form unfamiliar to me. It appeared to be an exact image, but as the negative of a photograph. As I looked more closely I realized there were differences. I only experienced this as the negative, but it was not a negative (or positive depending on how one looks at this). It was not a mirror image either, but it was clearly an inverse system, and contained within it all the dimensions, laws of physics, spiritual laws, and divine forces, but in their opposite form. It was not really possible to describe these anti-forces in any earthly terms, but the intensity was total. There were also star systems and stars and planets, but inverse, in as much as space appeared to be solid, and the spaces that were stars and planets appeared to be hollow. They were like holes in a cheese instead of spheres in spaces. The reality, however, was different, its appearance deriving from my way of thinking. In the inverse system, the empty spaces were real, and used as habitats by beings who lived on planets, which were for us empty spaces.

The angel said, "As you can see, all you know is present here, but the dimensions that determine its existence here are also present, although as negative values. The system you know is combined with this anti-system in a perfect balance, and together they are everything and nothing. Everything in your thinking, which is positive or negative, has its perfect complement here, and together they belong to the absolute God. Also, your own complement, your anti-soul, is here, as is that of everyone else."

I asked if was allowed to see this, but the angel said, "That is not allowed. It is not possible to meet each other until all the souls have completed their journey of evolution, and can enter the Kingdom of Heaven. Only there is it possible. The fact that you can now enter this system without problem is thanks to the fact that your inverse complement is on a journey through your system, with the help of the companion whom you left at the border of the anti-system. If this was not the case, you could not come here, because it is impossible for souls to be in each other's inverse field, as long as they are still in the process of evolution. Besides, your soul is still half, because you are not yet unified with your own soul's half in your own system. You see, it is very complicated."

I understood this and together we floated through the inverse system, watching all sorts of scenes, which were completely opposite from what I knew. Even the colors had their inverse image, but I could not describe them in familiar terms.

I had questions, but at this moment some of them were too complex to be answered. I understood, however, that each action and each fragment in our thinking had its opposite in this inverse system, and that everything was in complete balance.

The angel continued, "You have now seen the anti-forces and the inverse field. Yet this is still not everything. There are also anti-gods and anti-dragons. In short, everything you have seen has its inverse complement. Without this inverse system, there would be no movement, change, and evolution.

"Only the real and absolute God is above all. Learn this lesson and remember well, and every action you will undertake from now on, you can do with a new awareness."

We continued the journey, and I understood that I would learn no more for the moment. Slowly we arrived at the borderline, and I saw from afar that my faithful companion was waiting for me. I felt a slight trembling in the angel now beside me at the moment she saw the other angel, but otherwise nothing. As I passed the border, I felt very strange. It took some time before I felt normal, and I was thankful to look at something familiar – the system around me. It really felt good to be in back in the normal system.

The angel smiled and asked, "How was your journey?" I told her what I had experienced and she replied, "What you have seen is unique, but you can also understand that it is not easy to retain knowledge about this. Just be thankful that you were allowed to see this, and remember that the anti-forces exist. More than that is not permitted. I will bring you home now."

Impressed by this experience, I arrived back in my own surroundings.

Conclusion

In this book you have experienced issues that will undoubtedly raise many feelings, impressions, and questions. I would appreciate it if you would communicate those impressions and questions to me by e-mail to: jaap.hiddinga@btopenworld.com or by post directly to the publishers.